The Journal of Andrew Fuller Studies 8
Published in the United States of America
by The Andrew Fuller Center for Baptist Studies
The Southern Baptist Theological Seminary
2825 Lexington Road
Louisville, Kentucky 40280

© The Andrew Fuller Center for Baptist Studies 2024

All rights reserved. No part of this publication may be reproduced, stored in a retrieval system, or transmitted, in any form or by any means, without the prior permission in writing of The Andrew Fuller Center for Baptist Studies, or as expressly permitted by law, by license, or under terms agreed with the appropriate reproduction rights organization.

ISBN 978-1-77484-148-8

Printed by H&E Publishing, West Lorne, Ontario, Canada

The Journal of Andrew Fuller Studies

The Journal of Andrew Fuller Studies is an open access, double-blind peer-reviewed, scholarly journal published online biannually in the Spring and Fall by the Andrew Fuller Center for Baptist Studies (under the auspices of The Southern Baptist Theological Seminary). The publication language of the journal is English. Articles that deal with the life, ministry, and thought of the Baptist pastor-theologian Andrew Fuller are very welcome, as well as essays on his friends, his Particular Baptist community in the long eighteenth century (1680s–1830s), and the global impact of his thought, known as "Fullerism."

Articles and book reviews are to follow generally the style of Kate L. Turabian, *A Manual for Writers of Research Papers, Theses, and Dissertations*, 9th ed. (Chicago, IL: University of Chicago Press, 2018). They may be submitted in British, American, Australian, New Zealand, or Canadian English. Articles should be between 5,000 and 8,000 words, excluding footnotes. Articles are to be sent to the Editor and book reviews to the Book Review Editor.

Editor:
Michael A G Haykin, ThD, FRHistS
Professor of Church History
& Director, The Andrew Fuller Center for Baptist Studies
The Southern Baptist Theological Seminary, Louisville, Kentucky
mhaykin@sbts.edu

Associate editor:
Baiyu Andrew Song, PhD, FRAS
Adjunct Course Professor
Carey Theological College
Vancouver, BC
basong@carey-edu.ca

Design editor & Book review editor:
Caleb Anthony Neel, PhD cand.
The Southern Baptist Theological Seminary, Louisville, Kentucky
cneel@sbts.edu

Editorial board:
Cindy Aalders, DPhil
Director of the John Richard Allison Library
& Assistant Professor of the History of Christianity
Regent College, Vancouver

Dustin B. Bruce, PhD
Dean & Assistant Professor of Christian Theology and Church History
Boyce College
Louisville, Kentucky

Chris W. Crocker, PhD
Pastor, Markdale Baptist Church, ON
& Associate Professor of Church History
Toronto Baptist Seminary
Toronto, Ontario

Chris Chun, PhD
Professor of Church History & Director of the Jonathan Edwards Center
Gateway Seminary
Ontario, California

Jenny-Lyn de Klerk, PhD
Editor, Book Division
Crossway
Wheaton, Illinois

Jason G. Duesing, PhD
Provost & Professor of Historical Theology
Midwestern Baptist Theological Seminary
Kansas City, Missouri

Nathan A. Finn, PhD
Provost & Dean of the University Faculty
North Greenville University
Tigerville, South Carolina

C. Ryan Griffith, PhD
Pastor, Cities Church
St. Paul, Minnesota

Peter J. Morden, PhD
Principal
Bristol Baptist College
Clifton Down
Bristol, England

Adriaan C. Neele, PhD
Director, Doctoral Program & Professor of Historical Theology
Puritan Reformed Theological Seminary
Grand Rapids, Michigan
& Research Scholar
Yale University, Jonathan Edwards Center
New Haven, Connecticut

Robert Strivens, PhD
Pastor, Bradford on Avon Baptist Church (UK)
& Lecturer in Church History
London Seminary
London, England

Tom Nettles, PhD
Senior Professor of Historical Theology
The Southern Baptist Theological Seminary
Louisville, Kentucky

Blair Waddell, PhD
Pastor, Providence Baptist Church
Huntsville, Alabama

Contents

The Journal of Andrew Fuller Studies
No. 8, Spring 2024

Articles

Anne Dutton and Church Books: The importance of manuscript sources in reconstructing the lives of eighteenth-century Baptist women *Timothy Whelan*	9
The fall and rise of Benjamin Dutton: An early evangelical narrative of conversion and holiness *Matthew D. Haste*	26
A resurgence of Benjamin Beddome studies: A bibliographic essay *Yuta Seki*	44
John Fawcett on anger *Anna Carini*	60

Texts & documents

"Clipston Revival, July 10th 1800: An account & remarks of the revival in the congregation at Clipston derived from the Church Records" *ed. Sean Carter*	71
A Newly Discovered Letter from John Ryland, Jr. (1753–1825) to Christopher Anderson (1782–1852) *ed. Baiyu Andrew Song*	73

Book reviews — 85

Anne Dutton and Church Books: The importance of manuscript sources in reconstructing the lives of eighteenth-century Baptist women

Timothy Whelan

Timothy Whelan has published widely on British Religious Dissent of the Long 18th C. (especially among Baptists) and its intersections with women writers, print culture, and various Romantic figures, with many of these articles appearing in the *Baptist Quarterly* and various literary journals. He is the general editor of *Nonconformist Women Writers, 1720-1840* (8 vols., 2011); author of *Other British Voices: Women, Poetry, and Religion, 1766-1840* (2015); editor, with Michael McMullen, of *The Diary of Andrew* Fuller (2016); and creator of the website *Nonconformist and Dissenting Women's Studies*.

Despite being the most prolific woman writer of the eighteenth century, a complete accounting of Anne Dutton's life and publishing history has proved an elusive task. Until recently, most commentators have relied on Dutton's spiritual biography, *A Brief Account of the Gracious Dealings of God, with a Poor, Sinful, Unworthy Creature* (1743, 1750) and "An Account of the Gracious Dealings of God with Mrs. Anne Dutton in her Last Affliction, which Issued in her Death" (1769), the latter republished with additional information by J.A. Jones in "A Memoir of Mrs. Anne Dutton" (1833).[1] Fortunately, genealogical, bibliographical, and ecclesiastical materials are now more easily attained, enabling scholars to uncover details about Dutton that previously would have been possible only for those working in the

---

1 See Anne Dutton, *Letters on Spiritual Subjects, and Divers Occasions: Sent to Relations and Friends. By Mrs. Anne Dutton, Prepared for the Press by the Author, before her death, and now Published at her Desire; to which are Prefixed, Memoirs of the Dealings of God with her, in her last Sickness*, 2 vols (London: G. Keith, 1769); and idem, *A Narration of the Wonders of Grace, in Six Parts . . . To Which is added, a Poem on the Special Work of the Spirit in the Hearts of the Elect. Also, Sixty One Hymns composed on Several Subjects*, ed. J.A. Jones (London: John Bennett, 1833). Christopher Goulding's three prefaces to his reprints of works by Dutton in 1818, 1819, and 1823–24, provide a few details not present in the other accounts, but his proposed memoir of Dutton never appeared.

most advantageous situations.[2] As a result, commentators on Dutton can now speak with greater clarity and significance about her role as a biblical commentator and spiritual advisor to numerous Baptist and evangelical leaders as well as several congregations in England and America during the 1730s and 1740s.

Some of the obscurity surrounding Dutton's life and writings can be partially attributed to her title pages, of which only one bore her name during her lifetime, the first edition of *A Narration of the Wonders of Grace* (1734). Thereafter, her works were identified either by her initials (A. D.) or a variety of appellations, such as "One who has Tasted that the Lord is Gracious" (17 titles), "A Friend in the Country," "One that is less than the Least of them All, and Unworthy to be of their Happy Number," "A Sinner sav'd to be an Heir of Heaven, that deserves to be a Firebrand of Hell," "A Friend in England," and "One who is less than the least of all Saints." Though her name was effectively hidden after her initial publication, her gender was easily known after the publication of her spiritual autobiography, *A Brief Account of the Gracious Dealings of God, with a Poor, Sinful, Unworthy Creature* (1743), which also contained a meticulous account of her publications to that point. By the end of 1743 her fame as a writer (she published 17 titles that year), despite her attempts at anonymity, forced her to defend herself publicly in *Letter to such of the Servants of Christ, who may have any Scruple about the Lawfulness of Printing any thing written by a Woman* (1743), a stirring defense of her right as a Baptist woman to compose and publish religious treatises and spiritual letters. Her full name did not appear on another title page until 1769, when a posthumous edition of her *Letters* (containing the biographical "Account") was printed and sold by George Keith, the son-in-law of John Gill (1697–1771), Baptist minister at Horsleydown (later Carter Lane), Southwark. In the nineteenth century, reprints of works by Dutton rightly identified her on the title pages, usually accompanied with biographical accounts taken from Dutton's *A Brief Account* or Keith's "Account." She also appeared in five successive editions of *Memoirs of Eminently Pious Women* between 1804 and 1836. Oddly enough, the entry on Dutton in these volumes made no mention of her other titles and was guilty of several biographical inaccuracies, including the bizarre suggestion that she may have died shortly after her marriage at the age of 22.[3] Nevertheless, these efforts, despite their shortcomings, demonstrated, at least among the Baptists, a recognition that Dutton's legacy, although known only in a

---

2 For a complete calendar of the works of Anne Dutton, with images of her title pages, see Timothy Whelan, "Anne Dutton: Bibliography" at https://www.nonconformistwomenwriters1650-1850.com/anne-dutton-bibliography.

3 George Jerment, the editor of volume 2 in the 1804 edition of *Memoirs of Eminently Pious Women* (Thomas Gibbons compiled the initial volume in 1775), admits he does not know when she was born or where or when she died, and even invokes the stereotype of the "weaker vessel" by suggesting Dutton deserved to be "ranked with those instances of premature ripeness of character which God seems to honour by an early removal of the individual from a world of temptation and sorrow into the presence of their Lord." See Samuel Burder, ed., *Memoirs of Eminently Pious Women, of the British Empire*, 3 vols (London: J. Duncan, Longman and Co., Hatchard and Son, Seeley and Son, Hamilton, Adams, and Co., Simpkin and Marshall, and J. Nisbet, 1827), 2:227, 255.

fragmentary way, deserved to be noted and preserved.⁴

In the early decades of the twentieth century, Dutton's reputation diminished significantly as a result of scathing critiques of her work (and even her person) by her first biographer, J.C. Whitebrook, and two Baptist historians, W.T. Whitley and H. Wheeler Robinson.⁵ These men viewed her as a pretentious and vain woman committed to outworn tenets of strict Calvinism and an extreme form of conversion experience that, in her autobiographical writings, depicted her as a visionary, egotistical, overly emotional hindrance to mid-eighteenth-century evangelical efforts. Whitebrook and Robinson criticized the portraits which adorned many of her posthumous volumes, characterizing them as more representative of a "Court beauty" than a Baptist minister's wife, specifically noting her "shapely little head," "large curly ringlets," "well-poised neck," and "sprightly" expression that "explains much of the airiness which she laments."⁶ As late as 1961, Hugh Martin, a Baptist historian of the hymn, described Dutton as "a most eccentric creature" who aspired to become the first "female Pope" of the English Baptists; he pilloried her as a woman "[e]gotistical in the extreme and given to dressing in the most ostentatious way" (another reference to her published portraits).⁷ Fortunately, since the mid-1970s, the works of Stephen Stein, Susan Durden, Susan O'Brien, Michael Haykin, JoAnn Ford Watson, Michael Sciretti, and Huafang Xu have done much to restore the life and writings of Anne Dutton to their proper place within the religious, literary, and social history of eighteenth-century England.⁸

---

4 Besides Jones's edition of Dutton's *Narration of the Wonders of Grace* (1833), see *A Poem on the Special Work of the Spirit in the Hearts of the Elect. By the late Mrs. Anne Dutton* (London: Richard Baynes, 1818); *Letters on Spiritual Subjects. Sent to Relations and Friends. By the Late Mrs. Anne Dutton*, Parts I and II, ed. Christopher Goulding (London: T. Bensley, 1823, 1824); *A Poem on the Special Work of the Spirit in the Hearts of the Elect*, 4th edition, ... corrected [by C. G.] (Brighton, 1831); and *Selections from Letters on Spiritual Subjects: Addressed to Relatives and Friends*, ed. James Knight (London: John Gadsby, 1884).

5 John Cudworth Whitebrook, "A Bibliography of Mrs. Anne Dutton," *Notes and Queries* (December 1916): 471–73; idem, "The Life and Works of Mrs. Ann Dutton," *Transactions of the Baptist Historical Society* 7 (1921): 129–46; idem, *Ann Dutton: A Life and Bibliography* (London: A.W. Cannon, 1921); H. Wheeler Robinson, *The Life and Faith of the Baptists*, rev. ed. (1927, London: Kingsgate Press, 1946), 52–60; and W.T. Whitley, *A History of British Baptists* (London: Kingsgate Press, 1932), 214–15.

6 Whitebrook, *Life and Bibliography*, 6; the same passage from Whitebrook is quoted in Robinson, *Life and Faith*, 54.

7 Hugh Martin, "The Baptist Contribution to Early English Hymnody," *Baptist Quarterly* 19 (1961–62): 196. See also Peter Toon, *The Emergence of Hyper-Calvinism in English Nonconformity, 1689–1765* (London, England: Olive Tree, 1967), 149; Raymond Brown, *The English Baptists of the Eighteenth Century* (London: Baptist Historical Society, 1986), 79; and Peter Naylor, *Picking up a Pin for the Lord: English Particular Baptists from 1688 to the Early Nineteenth Century* (London: Grace Publications, 1992), 58.

8 See Stephen Stein, "Note on Anne Dutton, Eighteenth-Century Evangelical," *Church History* 44 (December 1975): 485–91; Barbara J. MacHaffie, *Her Story: Women in Christian Tradition* (Philadelphia: Fortress Press, 1986), 84–85; Susan Durden, "A Study of the First Evangelical Magazines, 1740–1748," *Journal of Ecclesiastical History* 27 (July 1976): 255–75; Susan O'Brien, "A Transatlantic Community of Saints: The Great Awakening and the First Evangelical Network, 1735–1755," *American Historical Review* 91 (1986): 811–32; JoAnn Ford Watson, "Anne Dutton: An Eighteenth Century British Evangelical Woman Writer," *Ashland Theological Journal* 30 (1998): 51–56; idem, ed., *Selected Spiritual Writings of Anne Dutton: Eighteenth-Cen-

Family Background and Early Marriages, 1692–1732
Anne Williams (her maiden name) was baptized at the All Saints Parish Church in Northampton on December 11, 1692.[9] At some point her family began attending the Independent congregation at Castle Hill during the ministry of John Hunt. She was converted in 1705 and joined the congregation two years later, having become by that time an avid reader of Joseph Hussey (1660–1726), high Calvinist Independent minister at Cambridge. After Hunt's departure from Castle Hill in 1708, Anne found the new minister, Thomas Tingey, unsatisfactory in regard to his theology and preaching and soon made her way to a Particular Baptist congregation led by John Moore (1662–1726) that was meeting in a house near what was then known as "the Watering Place." She joined the congregation in November 1710 prior to the congregation's move to a new chapel in College Lane (later College Street). She was baptized at some point during her time at College Lane, though no record of her baptism appears in the minutes of the church.[10] On January 4, 1715, she married Thomas Cattle (Cattel) (baptized June 7, 1691), a merchant originally from nearby Harlestone who was also a member at College Street.[11] The Cattles settled shortly thereafter in London. By August 1715, Anne was attending the Baptist meeting in Curriers' Hall, Cripplegate, led by John Skepp (1675–1721), a high Calvinist minister like Hunt, Hussey, and Moore. She became a transient member on October 1 of that year but did not join the congregation until March 31, 1718, at which time she gave "a Large & very Choice account of the Work of the Spirit of God on her Soule to the great Joy of the Church."[12] She was received into

---

tury, British-Baptist, Woman Theologian, 7 vols (Macon: Mercer University Press, 2003–2015); Michael A.G. Haykin, "Anne Dutton and Calvinistic Spirituality in the Eighteenth Century," *The Banner of Sovereign Grace Truth* (July/August 2002): 156–57; Michael D. Sciretti, "'Feed My Lambs': The Spiritual Direction Ministry of Calvinistic British Baptist Anne Dutton During the Early Years of the Evangelical Revival" (PhD diss., Baylor University, 2009); David H.J. Gay, *The Spirituality of Anne Dutton* (UK: Brachus Press, 2017); and Huafang Xu, "Communion with God and Comfortable Dependence on Him: Anne Dutton's Trinitarian Spirituality" (PhD diss., The Southern Baptist Theological Seminary, 2018).

9 Northamptonshire, England, Church of England Baptisms, Marriages and Burials, 1532–1812, Northampton, All Saints, Parish Registers, 1559–1722. Thomas Williams was listed as a "gardiner." This date, along with numerous other records from Dutton's life presented in this section, has not been previously known. The entry for Dutton by Karen O'Dell Bullock in the *Oxford Dictionary of National Biography* suggests her birth as either 1691 or 1692 and possibly 1695.

10 College Street Church Book, 1698–1737 (unpaginated), CSBC 45, Northamptonshire Record Office, Northampton. Dutton's *Brief Hints Concerning Baptism* (London: J. Hart, 1746) suggests that she was baptized in the Northampton church.

11 See Northamptonshire, England, Church of England Baptisms, Marriages and Burials, 1532–1812, Northampton, All Saints, Parish Registers, 1559–1722. Thomas Cattel [Cattle] sought admission to the congregation on April 8, 1713, but was not received by the church until December 16, 1713. See College Street Church Book, 1698–1737. The *ODNB* places Anne's marriage in 1714 to a man named "Cattel, or possibly Coles," the latter name being repeated by JoAnn Ford Watson in the Introduction to Volume 1 of her series, *Selected Spiritual Writings of Anne Dutton* (Macon: Mercer University Press, 2004), xv–xvi.

12 Curriers' Hall, Cripplegate, Church Book, 1692–1723, Angus Library, Regent's Park College, Oxford,

full communion on April 6, 1718. For whatever reason, her husband never joined at Cripplegate and she said little about him in her *Brief Account*. At some point his business took him to Warwick, where she felt her spiritual situation decline. The Cattles soon returned to London, whereupon Thomas Cattle died during or before the early months of 1719 (no death record has yet surfaced). Anne returned to Northampton as a young widow to live once again with her parents and attend at College Street.

If the assumed date of the death of Thomas Cattle is correct (early 1719), then Anne wasted little time in erasing her widowhood, for on November 2 of that year she married Benjamin Brown Dutton (1691/2–1747) at the All Saints Parish Church in Northampton.[13] Given the protocols at that time for remarriage, placing the date of the death of her first husband prior to 1719 seems more apropos, though that date cannot be known with certainty. Benjamin Dutton was the son of the Baptist minister at Eversholt (also spelled "Evershalt"), Bedfordshire. In his youth he was apprenticed to a draper and clothier in Newbury and experienced his conversion there, an event that led to his call to the ministry in 1709. He spent much of the next decade studying under ministers in Buckinghamshire, Westmoreland, Scotland, and London. A few weeks after the death of his father on August 11, 1719, he moved to Northampton to continue his preparations for the ministry, this time under the tutelage of John Moore at College Street. Benjamin met Anne shortly thereafter and in less than three months they were married. He had little to say about her in his spiritual autobiography but his statement upon first seeing her would prove prophetic: "I was much taken with her Christian Discourse, and had this Thought pass'd through my Mind, that she would make a brave Minister's Wife."[14] She indeed possessed both qualities and demonstrated them fully in the 1740s and 1750s.

Upon Benjamin's arrival in London to study for the ministry, he joined the Baptist congregation at Maze Pond (the church book records his name as "Benjamin Dunton") on March 12, 1716. Thus, for much of the period between 1716 and 1719, Anne and Benjamin resided in London and attended two of London's most prominent Baptist churches, though there is no record that they ever met during that time. Benjamin was later censured by Maze Pond for falling

fols 93v., 106v. Sciretti found the marriage certificate and thus corrected both accounts ("Feed my Lambs," 66, n. 65).

13 Northamptonshire, England, Church of England Baptisms, Marriages and Burials, 1532–1812, Northampton, St. Sepulchre, Parish Registers, 1566–1723. Benjamin writes in his spiritual autobiography that his marriage occurred in his 28th year, meaning he had not yet celebrated his 28th birthday as we refer to it today; thus, his birth could have been in late 1691 but most likely occurred in 1692, making him only slightly older than Anne. No birth record has surfaced, a common occurrence among Particular Baptists who did not baptize or christen infants. See Benjamin Dutton, *The Superaboundings of the Exceeding Riches of God's Free-Grace, towards the Chief of the Chief of Sinners. Shewn forth in the Lord's Gracious Dealings with that Poor, Unworthy, Hell-deserving Worm, Benjamin Dutton: Minister of the Gospel, and Pastor of a Church of Christ, at Great Gransden, Huntingdonshire* (London: J. Hart, 1743), 129.

14 Dutton, *Superaboundings of the Exceeding Riches of God's Free-Grace*, 129.

into an unspecified sin (most likely his overuse of alcohol, which continued to afflict him into the late 1720s). After much soul searching and repentance, driven by the death of his father, his removal to Northampton, and his marriage to Anne, he applied for a letter of dismission from Maze Pond in 1721. The church declined his application, but the following year believed his repentance sufficiently sincere to grant his dismission on June 21, 1722:

> B^r Benj: Dunton having sent divers Letters to signifie his Repentance (and the Church having several intimations of the truth of it;) and owning likewise the justness of the Churches proceedings with him; entreats them to remove their censure. Which is granted. And the Church ^appoints^ B^r Edwd Wallin, and B^r Carter to signifie the same to the Church, that he would sit down with; and that we give him up to their care; if they are satisfied with his late Conversation desiring them if they take him in, to give us notice thereof, the first opportunity.[15]

The church that he "would sit down with" was not the congregation in College Street, however, but rather a nearby church, as he notes in his autobiography, most likely the church at Wellingborough led by William Grant.[16] From this church Benjamin Dutton was commissioned to preach sometime around 1724. A year later, he began a three-year stint as a supply minister at small congregations in Whittlesey and Wisbech, Cambridgeshire. By 1728 the Duttons had returned to Wellingborough. Not long thereafter Benjamin began assisting Benjamin Winkles at Arnesby, Leicestershire, and accordingly moved his membership to that congregation.

Though Benjamin experienced difficulties and delays in receiving a proper dismission from Maze Pond, Anne surprisingly never sought dismission from the Cripplegate congregation until 1728, joining Grant's congregation at Wellingborough that year after a nine-year absence from the London congregation. The church book for Cripplegate does not note her departure in 1719, nor is she ever listed among the list of transient or dismissed members there through 1723, the year the church book closes. In fact, the Curriers' Hall church book includes her among the members in attendance at the annual meetings of the church on May 3, 1719, and May 1, 1720, the second entry listing her as "Anne Cattle" despite having been married to Dutton for about six months. In the entry for May 7, 1721, she appears as "Ann Dutton once Cattle." She even paid 5 shillings toward the church's debt in 1720.[17] Neither does the College Street church book list her as a transient member from Cripplegate, though she referred to herself in such terms during her

---

15 Maze Pond Church Book, Vol. 3, 1713–22, Angus Library, Regent's Park College, Oxford, unpaginated.

16 Dutton, *Superaboundings of the Exceeding Riches of God's Free-Grace*, 129. Benjamin Dutton does not name the church, but says it was about five miles from Northampton, and from Anne's record of the events in *A Brief Account*, it would appear that they left Northampton for Wellingborough around 1723.

17 Curriers' Hall, Cripplegate, Church Book, 1692–1723, Angus Library, Regent's Park College, Oxford, fols 115v., 125v., 133v., and 126v.

time in Great Gransden, as recorded in a brief account of her death in the Great Gransden church book.[18] Why she chose not to rejoin at College Street is unclear, but it may have had something to do with her lack of enthusiasm for the preaching of John Moore. At Wellingborough, however, her appreciation for the ministry of William Grant was immediate and lasting; she corresponded with him often and valued him as one of her primary spiritual advisors.[19]

In 1731, Benjamin Dutton quit his work at Arnesby and began preaching to the Baptist meeting in Great Gransden. After much soul-searching on Anne's part, she agreed to leave Wellingborough with her husband and settle at Great Gransden. A year later they applied for membership, with Benjamin's letter of dismission coming oddly enough not from the church at Arnesby but rather his father's old congregation at Eversholt (he did not provide an explanation for this discrepancy in his spiritual autobiography). Anne's letter of dismission came from the Wellingborough church and was inserted into the church book along with her husband's letter. Benjamin joined on 22 June, 1732, and was ordained that October; Anne joined on December 3, 1732, the last Baptist congregation she would join.[20]

Dutton's Role in Church Leadership at Great Gransden, 1732–1765

Though she composed a few works prior to 1732, Anne Dutton's life for the first thirteen years of her marriage was largely circumscribed by her husband's work in Wellingborough, Whittlesey, Wisbech, Arnsby, and Great Gransden. By 1743, however, the year he sailed for America on a preaching tour to raise funds for an addition to the chapel as well as to promote his wife's writings, Anne Dutton stood at the forefront of her most productive period, having published 28 titles by the end of that year and established herself as a prominent figure within the Evangelical Revival movement in Great Britain and America. Her publications provided Dutton with a tangible outlet for what she believed to be her "calling" as a theological commentator and spiritual advisor to ministers and laypersons at home and abroad. Her role as a pastor's wife was also a part of that calling. As she writes in *A Brief Account*, "In a Word, I thought my great Lord, had Work to do at G-----n, that my dear Yokefellow was call'd to go as an *upper* Servant, and myself as *under One* to attend him. And I saw such a Glory in my *Lord's Work*, that I esteem'd

---

18 An entry shortly after Dutton's death in November 1765 notes that "She was a transient member of the church of as she says Mr Sk—p at L—n." See Great Gransden Church Book, 1694-1772 (non-paginated), Huntingdonshire Record Office, FR6/1/1.

19 Dutton writes of her experience at Wellingborough: "And here I may take Notice, that before my going to W----- [Wisbech], I had a Desire to join with the Church of Christ at W----h [Wellingborough], over which Mr. G----t [Grant] was Pastor. Upon which I sought the Lord to acquaint me with his Mind therein. ... Upon this, I wrote for my Dismission from the Church at L----n [London], to which I belong'd, to the Church at W-----h, aforesaid. ... Which accordingly came to pass. For upon my being brought back again, and restored to all my former Privileges, as aforesaid, I had this additional one granted, of being *join'd to the Church*, and enjoying a full and most delightful Communion with that Company of favoured Saints" (Dutton, *Brief Account*, 2:130-31).

20 Dutton, *Superaboundings of the Exceeding Riches of God's Free-Grace*, 102. There is no record that the Duttons ever lived at Evershalt after their marriage.

it an unspeakable Dignity and Privilege, to be employ'd in the *least* Part of it."²¹

Whatever her duties had been previous to his departure for America, upon learning the news of his death in 1747 (the ship floundered on its return to England), Anne Dutton quickly assumed a new role that had previously fallen within the purview of her husband. Though she never desired to preach from the pulpit at Great Gransden, she was not averse to attending the church meetings in her husband's absence and, at some point in 1749, took it upon herself to compose all the entries in the Great Gransden church book covering the years 1743 through 1759. For a Particular Baptist woman to compose the entries in the church book at this time, a task usually performed by the minister or a deacon, would have been viewed only slightly below a woman preaching to the congregation, both acts perceived as violations of the Pauline requirement for women to be silent in the church and not to usurp authority over men (1 Cor 14:34–35 and 1 Tim 2:12). In this instance, however, the small congregation at Great Gransden made no attempt to stop Dutton from maintaining the church book. In so doing, she earned the distinction of being the *only* Baptist woman to act in such a capacity in the eighteenth century, an achievement revealed now for the first time, further strengthening her position as one of the most remarkable Baptist women of her day.²²

The entries in the church book, though unsigned, bear all the hallmarks of Dutton's handwriting as well as her style and sentiments, the latter qualities having been demonstrated at length in her letters and other writings. Her first entry begins in August 1743 but was probably written in September 1749, for it is a continuous narrative that recounts her husband's departure for America, his fundraising and evangelistic work there (she notes that his preaching led to the "Conversion of Eleven, or Twelve Souls"), his unfortunate demise ("he was cast away by Sea," she writes), and the subsequent state of the small orphaned congregation in Great Gransden. By September of 1749 the church was in a perilously low estate, both in spirit and in numbers, a great concern to Dutton. Near the end of that month, however, the church acquired the services of David Evans from Hook Norton. Dutton's anxiety and joy were evident in her entry for that month:

> Our Distress was very great, as we could not get Supplies, & had no Prospect how we could keep up ye Meeting during ye Winter. But when ye Night was darkest, ye Day began to dawn. The Lord, whose Mercy endureth forever,

---

21 Dutton, *Brief Account* (Part II), 153.

22 Great Gransden [Baptist] Church Book, 1694–1777, Huntingdonshire Archives, KFR6/1/1. The section in the church book completed by Dutton, from which all quotations in this essay are derived, suggests that her presence at the church meetings may have exceeded that of a casual hearer from among the congregation. It is not improbable that the church book resided in her home since it was often the minister who recorded the entries in the book. All further references to Dutton's entries are from this unpaginated section of the church book. For the complete transcription of these entries, as well as some images from the church book, see Timothy Whelan, "Anne Dutton Entries in the Great Gransden Church Book" at https://www.nonconformistwomenwriters1650-1850.com/biographical-summaries/dutton-anne-1692-1765/anne-dutton-entries-in-the-great-grandson-church-book.

remembred us in our low Estate, & sent his dear Servant, Mr. Evans, to reside amongst us & minister to us, at a Time untho't of, to our pleasing Surprize, he being before unknown to us.

Dutton's relief at this turn of events is palpable, noting that "This great Mercy, as it was a rich Supply of our present Necessity, we receiv'd with Thanksgiving, as an Answer of Prayer."

Prior to Evans's arrival, however, Dutton's prayers had actually been for a different minister. Not only was Dutton occupied with her duties at church meetings and composing entries in the church book but she had also taken an active role in procuring her own choice of a minister for the congregation. Stephen Addington (1729–1796) was studying at that time at Philip Doddridge's (1702–1751) academy in Northampton, Dutton's home village. Doddridge was not only a prominent Dissenting educator but also the minister at the Independent meeting in Castle Hill, the same congregation in which Dutton had been converted and where her relations still attended and where Addington had most likely attended since his youth. Dutton writes that before Evans's arrival, the church had been in "a divided State," a reference to the congregation's departure in the mid-1730s, during the ministry of Benjamin Dutton, from their original position on closed communion to a more open position in which those who had been baptized as infants could become members provided their profession of faith was acceptable to the congregation. The primary reason behind the change appears to have been less doctrinal and more practical, for given the low number of members in the congregation, an open communion could allow for local people to join whose doctrinal positions as Independents were nearly identical to those of most Particular Baptists, aside from baptism. Dutton was clearly a practitioner of believer's baptism, having published a lengthy treatise on the subject in 1746, but her position on closed or open communion may have fluctuated at times.[23] Whatever the case, her aggressive recruiting of Addington through a series of letters to Doddridge makes clear that she was not entirely averse to having an Independent paedobaptist minister overseeing the Particular Baptist meeting at Great Gransden.[24]

Dutton may have known of Addington from his youth in Northampton, and she may have met him on visits to her family during the 1730s and 1740s. In her three letters to Doddridge between June and September 1749, she implored him to send Addington to Great Gransden at his earliest convenience or at the latest

---

23 See Dutton's *Brief Hints concerning Baptism: of the Subject, Mode, and End of this Solemn Ordinance. In a Letter to a Friend. To which is added, A Short Account, how the Author was brought to follow the Lord in His Ordinance of Baptism. In a Letter to another Friend* (London: J. Hart, 1746).

24 Mixed congregations were not uncommon among Dissenters in the eighteenth century. Two of the more prominent examples were the Bunyan Meeting in Bedford (which for more than a century from its inception alternated between Baptist and Independent ministers) and Broadmead in Bristol, which accommodated its paedobaptist members by forming in 1757 a separate Independent congregation (called the "Little Church") that existed side by side with the Baptist congregation, with both congregations led by the same minister, always a Particular Baptist.

by Michaelmas (September 29), "if the Lord inclines y^r Heart to give him to us," she writes that August.[25] The gravity of her congregation's situation compelled her to a point of near bribery, proposing to Doddridge in her postscript that young Addington could use her husband's library as his own, which "w^d be a great advantage to him, as it w^d save him the charge of buying a Study of Books." She hopes Doddridge will agree, for if he sends Addington to another place, he will arrive there "naked as it were, & destitute of Helps." Doddridge replied to Dutton (the letter is not extant), informing her that he would keep Addington with him in Northampton for the time being, but if the congregation remained without a pastor into the following summer, that he would most likely send him at that time. Her next letter, on September 25, welcomed Doddridge's "kindness" to her "little Remnant" at Great Gransden, having known from the beginning that Doddridge had designed his young protégée "for a larger people." What ye Lord then wrought in your Heart," she declared, "you will find recorded in His & written for a Reward of Grace, to your endless Glory, in the book of his Remembrance," but her exuberant praise may have been partially designed to soften Doddridge's heart (or inflict it with guilt) through a third round of impassioned pleas to him to send Addington to minister to her "little Remnant," for "however needful Mr. A—n's stay with you may be, by reason of our pressing necessity, it prov'd trying, very trying to me." Once again, the immediate answer to her prayers had been postponed, causing her to confess that "Unbelief easily besets me in straits & difficulties," though, as "an unworthy, vile Creature," she recognizes that God would be fully justified "to take no notice of me." Nor is Doddridge obligated to her, though she cannot help but remind him that, in her present situation, "I know not how, Sir, we can get Supplies to keep up ye meeting, during the Winter." Nevertheless, his reluctance to help and her lack of faith will eventually yield to God's providential power, for "ye lord can carry us thro', tho' we see not how." At this point, Dutton the spiritual advisor and prolific author cannot refrain from offering counsel to her male counterpart, the eminently pious tutor, minister, and author of *The Rise and Progress of Religion in the Soul* (1745): "It is our Glory, Sir, to trust the Lord in ye Dark; & God accounts it his Glory, to bring his believing People forth to ye Light. And, O astonishing Grace! When He doth it, he pardons & passeth by all their Unbelief, & records & rewards their Faith, & tells of it to their Honour, that thereby they wrought Wonders!" The next day (September 26), Dutton added a second postscript to her letter, still pushing back somewhat on Doddridge's denial of her request by suggesting that she might write to Addington on her own and ask him if he could "serve us one Lord's Day in three Months, till he may come to reside among us," hoping he could

---

25 Dutton's letters to Doddridge can be found at Dr. Williams's Library, London, New College Collection, MS L1/5/65, 65a, and 66, dated January 30, 1743/44, [August 7], 1749, and September 25/26, 1749. The letter from June 1749 that Dutton mentions in her August letter is not extant. Her September letter confirms her brother's membership in Doddridge's congregation, noting that "It grieves my heart, y^t our Lord's Honour is wounded, by my poor Br. And an additional grief it is to me, y^t you, Sir, who watch for his soul, instead of having Joy in, have grief by him. O may ye Lord pity & restore him! I have lately wrote to him on ye Head."

begin on October 15th, but only if Doddridge concurs.

Doddridge did not concur, for his plans for Addington centered upon an Independent congregation at Spaldwick, Huntingdonshire, where Addington the following year commenced his ministerial career. Whether Doddridge made this clear to Dutton in his response to her September letter (another letter no longer extant) is unknown, but her applications to him ceased immediately, as indicated in her entry in the church book about the providential call of David Evans at the end of that September and the subsequent renewal of the original church covenant and its policy of closed communion. Whether that decision emerged from her own desire to restore church order or as a form of rebuke to her efforts to engage Addington as minister is unclear, for we cannot be certain that other members of the congregation were even aware of her efforts on behalf of Addington, for she never mentions it in the church book. In either case, her subsequent entries about the controversy over communion show no evidence of any disagreement on her part with the original covenant, even though it had been changed to an open position during the ministry of her husband. As she writes on December 2, 1749:

> We had a Church meeting; and those of us whose Hearts the Lord inclin'd to follow him in his Ordinances, humbled ourselves before him, intreated his forgiving Love, & his returning unto us with Mercies. This done, we renewed our solemn Covenant; in hopes y^t our other Brethren & Sisters, wch at present stood at a Distance, might in a little time come in & renew Covenant with us. And after this, ye same Day, Mr. Evans was received into our Communion, to our Heart's Joy, & ye Lord's Praise.

Evans accepted the church's call on January 5, 1750, and was set apart for his ministry there on February 27, 1750, a service led by William Wills, the minister at Benjamin Dutton's home church in Eversholt, suggesting a connection with the two churches that may have begun with Benjamin Dutton and was now being continued by his widow. Anne Dutton had high hopes for Evans, closing her entry for the service with a fervent prayer for God's power to fall upon the struggling congregation at Great Gransden: "And now, Lord, what wait we for? Our Eyes are upon THEE: Let thy great Blessing descend upon us, for the Advancement of ye Interest of our great Redeemer amongst us! Let thy Hand be with us; and many believe & turn unto ye Lord!"

Unfortunately, disagreements soon arose between Evans and the church and they parted ways in the fall of 1751, once again creating an absence of pastoral leadership in the small congregation, a situation that Dutton, however, steadfastly resigned to a sovereign God who, through the labors of previous ministers (including her husband) had "laid ye Foundation of a Work, in raising this little Church from its low Estate, which his own Hand will finish by another Instrument.--Oh y^t ye Lord would soon send us ye Man y^t he has chosen, & designs to use for ye Conversion of Sinners & Addition of Members: that his Name may be glorify'd & ye church edified! Lord Jesus, say Amen!" Thomas Ward was that man, replacing Evans in December 1751, upon which Dutton writes in her effusive yet heart-felt manner: "Thanks be to God, for ye Dawn of another Day, after a dark Night! And, Oh that thro' his Ministry, the Sun of Righteousness may arise upon us, wth Healing in his Wings!--Lord Jesus, let ye Times of Refreshing, come upon us from thy Presence!" By the following November, however, Ward had departed and was replaced by David Chapman from Walgrave.

Chapman was succeeded in October 1755 by Timothy Keymer, though he did not accept the formal call from the church until October 1758, with his ordination occurring that December. During all this pastoral turmoil, Dutton steadfastly maintained the church book, noting that Keymer's delay was occasioned by hopes the church's membership would increase before offering a formal commitment to him as the stated minister. She writes on October 29, 1758: "The Church had long desert'd getting into Order in Hope of others joining wth us: But as none were inclin'd to it, in our low Estate, we tho't it our Duty to proceed without them & in y^t way to wait for ye Lord' gracious Appearance in adding to us." Anne Dutton continued to enter the minutes in the Church Book through December 1759, four years after the arrival of Keymer, a further indication of the unusual nature of her activities in the church after the departure of her husband in 1743. Whether these activities by Dutton played any role in the short tenures of Evans, Wills, and Chapman is uncertain, though her obvious position as a prominent leader in the church (and keeper of the church book) may not have sat well with these ministers and their opinions of the proper role of women in the church. Nevertheless, her final entry in the church book—"And the Lord was with us"—composed on December 25, 1759, forms a fitting capstone not only to her prominent position at the church meeting that day but also her overriding concern for the church's spiritual health and continued prosperity, both of which allowed Dutton to experience a form of pastoral ministry not shared by any other Baptist woman of the eighteenth century.[26]

As with her numerous publications, so with her activities on behalf of the church, all were performed in full confidence that she was exercising her spiritual gifts as one of God's chosen vessels commissioned to provide spiritual guidance to individuals and congregations whenever and wherever the need arose. Her activities between 1743 and 1759 were in many ways a fulfilment of Benjamin

---

26 The year her husband left for America Dutton published a powerful defense of her right as a woman to publish her letters and religious discourses, many of which evidenced her role as a spiritual advisor to various individuals and congregations as well as that of a religious commentator or polemicist. Dutton's *Letter to such of the Servants of Christ* argued that her work as an author was "Lawful and Right" and did not run counter to Paul's strictures, which she believed applied only to women speaking *in public* to members of both sexes about matters of religion and not to women who spoke about such matters *in private*. See Anne Dutton, *A Letter to such of the Servants of Christ, who may have any Scruple about the Lawfulness of Printing any thing written by a Woman: to shew, that Book-teaching is Private, with respect to the Church, and permitted to private Christians; yea, commanded to those, of either sex, who are gifted for, and inclin'd to engage in this Service* (London: J. Hart, 1743), 3, 4.

Dutton's prediction of her after their initial meeting in 1719: "she would make a brave Minister's Wife."[27] Dutton remained at Great Gransden and continued to write and publish until her death on November 18, 1765, a date that has been incorrectly noted since 1769, when George Keith, in his "Account" of her last days, mistakenly noted that she died on Monday, November 17, 1765.[28] As the calendar for 1765 makes clear, that Monday was actually the 18th, not the 17th of November, a date that was entered correctly in four places in the Great Gransden Church Book--twice in a list of church members and the other two in brief notices of her death.[29]

Dutton's Bible and Anne Steele of Broughton

In her letter on August 7, 1749, Anne Dutton informed Doddridge that she planned to leave her books and those of her husband to the Great Gransden church "for ye use of ye Minister & Ministers of y^s Congregation successively, after my decease," a bequest of some 200 volumes that was dutifully fulfilled. One of the volumes in her library was a 1698 edition of the King James Bible by John Canne (the first edition appeared in 1647), a book that now resides in the Broughton Church Collection (10/1) at the Angus Library, Regent's Park College, Oxford. Hugh Martin implied that this Bible did not go to the church but rather was bequeathed directly by Dutton to Anne Steele, a claim that had been made prior to Martin's essay and repeated often thereafter.[30] The 1698 Canne Bible definitely came into the possession of Steele, and remained with her family until it came into the possession of the Broughton Church.[31] In the mid-twentieth century the church's library was loaned for a time to the Angus Library, with a few items remaining in the Angus today, one of which is the Dutton-Steele Bible.

If Martin's claim about this particular Bible is correct, it would indeed have been a remarkable gift and act of recognition by Anne Dutton, the most prolific

---

27 Dutton, *Superaboundings of the Exceeding Riches of God's Free-Grace*, 129.

28 Dutton, *Letters on Spiritual Subjects* (1769), xxvi.

29 Keith's "Account" notes that she "finished her Course at Great Gransden, Huntingdonshire, on Monday the 17th of November 1765, in the 74th Year of her Age" (*Letters on Spiritual Subjects*, 1.xxvi). The *ODNB* entry for Dutton repeats that date, as have all other accounts on Dutton.

30 Martin, "Baptist Contribution," 197. This was also noted by Cynthia Aalders in 2008: "Of particular interest here is a possible connection between Steele and Dutton. The Angus Library at Regent's Park College, Oxford contains a Bible which has been inscribed by first Dutton and then Steele. ... Early twentieth-century efforts, archived in the Angus Library, to ascertain the nature of their relationship were inconclusive, though Reuben Heffer surmises that "probably they knew each other by correspondence" (Cynthia Y. Aalders, *To Express the Ineffable: The Hymns and Spirituality of Anne Steele* [Milton Keynes, UK: Paternoster, 2008], 55–56, n97).

31 According to an early historian of the Broughton church, Steele's "Bible, which is a precious relic, is reserved in the minister's library at Broughton, and bears the name of another lady, who is not so well known in the church, *Anne Dutton*, to whom it appears once to have belonged. *W. Steele, jun.*, son of the pastor, left house and garden for the use of the minister," a reference that makes no mention of the Bible being bequeathed to Steele by Dutton. See Edward Compton, *A History of the Baptist Church, Broughton, Hampshire, from the year 1653 to the Present Time, Compiled from the Old Church Books* (Leicester: Winks and Son, 1878), 17.

Baptist woman writer in England prior to 1760, to Anne Steele (1717–1778), one of the most popular Baptist women writers after that date. A closer examination of the Bible, however, suggests that this was not the case. The volume does not appear to have ever been used as a personal Bible by Dutton or anyone else, for the volume is tightly bound with the pages pristine and unmarked except for a few at the beginning of the Bible. Nor are there any annotations in the Bible that would suggest a direct connection between Dutton and Steele.[32] Some pencilled scribblings in shorthand can be found on the inside of the front and back covers, but they appear to have been added later in an unknown hand. A portion of Canne's original preface copied onto one page is also not in Dutton's hand. The handwritten annotations at the front of the Bible have generally been considered the primary source that connects this particular Bible with these two women, but these annotations were not written by Dutton or Steele. Only Steele's signature ("Anne Steele Junr") situated in the middle of that page is authentic. The comments about Dutton and Steele were composed in an unknown hand sometime after the death of Anne Steele on November 11, 1778 (the date appears on the page) by a member of Steele's family or someone associated with the Broughton church after the Bible came to reside there. Dutton's name is spelled "Ann," and not "Anne," which is the spelling she used for her signature on her first publication in 1734 and in her surviving manuscript letters as well as the Great Gransden church book. More important, the date of her death is given as 17 November 1765, the incorrect date taken from Keith's "Account" in 1769.

Despite the lack of concrete evidence directly linking the Bible to Anne Dutton, the claim that the Bible once resided in the library of Anne and Benjamin Dutton prior to its possession by Anne Steele appears to be correct, but Steele's possession of the Bible was not the result of a direct action on the part of Dutton. By 1765 Dutton would most likely have had some knowledge of Steele's *Poems on Subjects Chiefly Devotional* (1760) and Steele would probably have known about Dutton's collection of hymns affixed to her *Narration of the Wonders of Grace* (1734) and *A Discourse Concerning the New Birth* (1743). Even though they were both accomplished Baptist women writers, no letters by Dutton to Steele appear in any of Dutton's numerous volumes of correspondence published during her lifetime or in the 1769 posthumous edition, nor has any mention of Anne Dutton surfaced to date in Steele's correspondence or letters by any of her family members now residing within the Steele Collection in the Angus Library.[33] Any letters that passed between them would have been cherished by each woman and possibly shared with (and preserved by) friends and relations. If Steele had acquired the Bible on a visit to Great Gransden, it seems feasible some mention of the event would have

---

32 The idea of bequeathing a personal Bible to someone else may well have been foreign to most Baptists at that time. Little, if any evidence, exists for such a practice outside of a family Bible remaining within the family.

33 For the complete text of all of Anne Steele's correspondence, see Julia B. Griffin, ed., *Anne Steele, Miscellaneous Pieces in Verse and Prose* (1780), *Verses for Children* (1788), *and Unpublished Poetry, Prose and Correspondence of Anne Steele*, vol. 1 of *Nonconformist Women Writers, 1720–1840* (London: Pickering & Chatto, 2011).

found its way into a letter or possibly the diary of her stepmother, Anne Cator Steele (1689–1760).[34] Such a visit by Steele seems unlikely, however, for by the 1760s her weak constitution and frequent bouts of illness would have made the journey from Hampshire to Huntingdonshire extremely difficult. The same would have been true for Dutton, who travelled little if any in her later years.

The more likely source for the Bible's eventual journey from Great Gransden to Broughton and eventually to Anne Steele is John Collins (c.1740s–1816), a book collector and antiquarian from nearby Devizes who appears to be the same John Collins who in 1765 joined the Broughton congregation where Anne Steele worshiped.[35] As a Baptist (most likely he was a relation, possibly the son, of a John Collins who ministered to a Baptist meeting in Devizes in the 1770s), Collins most likely knew of Dutton and her work and, as a book collector, would have been eager to acquire something she had once owned. He may have acquired it directly from Dutton while she was alive, or after her death in 1765, possibly as a gift from Dutton but more likely through a sale of some of her books after her death when they came into the possession of the Great Gransden church. It would appear that Collins's initial interest in obtaining something belonging to Dutton was probably based upon his own interests as a collector, for the inside cover bears his personal bookplate--"John Collins, Devizes." Had he been commissioned by Anne Steele to acquire something from the estate of Anne Dutton, it seems unlikely he would have affixed his bookplate to the volume, an act that nearly always exhibited personal ownership of a book. If this John Collins was the same who joined the Broughton church, then it seems probable that Anne Steele may have learned of his acquisition of the Bible through conversations with him and expressed an interest in acquiring the book for herself probably for the same reason he had acquired it--out of respect for the memory of a talented Baptist woman writer. Collins may have sold the volume to Steele, but it is more probable that he presented it to her as a gift, which she promptly signed and placed in her private library.

Information that the Bible once belonged to Anne Dutton probably originated with Collins, whose acquisition, whether directly from Dutton or the Great Gransden church, would have entitled him to a degree of inside knowledge about

---

34 The surviving volumes of her diary can be found in the Steele Collection, 2/1/1–3, Angus Library, Regent's Park College, Oxford. Selections from her diary can be found in Whelan, ed., *Nonconformist Women Writers*, 8:43–74.

35 Collins became a member of the Broughton church where Anne Steele worshiped in 1765, the year Dutton died. Most likely he was the son of John Collins, also of Devizes, who preached for several years in the 1770s to a congregation of Baptists there and who was known to the Steeles through their relations, the Attwaters, who themselves had relations through marriage with the Collinses. It is possible that both father and son were antiquarians, but the portrait now held among the collections at Yale would seem to suggest by its date (c.1799) that he is the John Collins who was a member at Broughton and died in 1816, possibly maintaining his business in Devizes during those years. Some helpful biographical notes by Paul Fiddes on Collins and his commonplace book (which also resides in the Angus Library) can be found in the Broughton Church Collection, Angus Library, Regent's Park College, Oxford. For references to a Rev. Collins of Devizes in Jane Attwater's diary, see Whelan, ed., *Nonconformist Women Writers*, 8:216. His portrait by John Russell (1745–1806) can be found at the Yale Center for British Art, Paul Mellon Collection, acc. no. B1977.14.6261. For his membership at the Broughton Church on September 12, 1765, see Broughton Church Book, from the year 1759, Broughton Church Collection 1/4, Angus Library, Regent's Park College, Oxford.

the Bible that would have been unavailable to anyone else in Broughton. Once established by Collins, the narrative that the Bible had previously belonged to Dutton would have been easily perpetuated by Steele and other members of the Broughton church after the volume came into the church's possession. If the narrative had been false, Collins would have had ample time to debunk it, for he did not die until 1816, almost forty years after Anne Steele's death. The handwritten notes about Dutton and Steele on the page that bears Steele's signature were probably added by a church member at that time, reinforcing a connection between the two women that later historians, apparently unaware of Collins's personal bookplate and Dutton's own handwriting, embellished into a symbolic passing of the literary mantle from one Baptist woman to another through the bequeathing of an old Bible.

The fact that John Collins the antiquarian book collector acquired a Bible from the personal library of Anne Dutton and gave or sold it to Anne Steele is not as compelling a thought as the claim that Dutton had bequeathed the Bible directly to Steele, but it is nevertheless a significant event in its own right. Collins's bookplate and Steele's signature not only illuminate an antiquarian's ability to acquire such a book and a poet's pleasure in receiving it, but also, and more importantly, the process negotiated by an unmarried provincial woman like Steele in order to gain a treasure that once belonged to another woman writer. Thus, Steele's acceptance of the Bible and placement of her signature suggests a recognition not only of Collins' esteem for Dutton and herself but also of her corresponding avowal of the importance of Dutton's place in the development of a vibrant tradition of Baptist women writers and hymnodists, a recognition that, despite long-standing accounts to the contrary, was never dependent upon a direct gift from Dutton to Steele.

Though Anne Dutton has experienced a significant rehabilitation in the past few decades for her role as a spiritual advisor and religious writer among the Baptists and evangelicals in Great Britain and America from the 1730s through the 1760s, she still deserves closer attention by scholars, especially in extricating previously unknown details about her life and activities as a Baptist woman and minister's wife and in providing closer readings and broader assessments of her substantial canon of publications. Such efforts will not only enhance her reputation as the most prolific woman writer among all Dissenting denominations during her lifetime but also cement her position as the central figure in a vibrant tradition of Baptist women writers of the long eighteenth century who composed personal narratives, poems, hymns, letters, meditations and religious treatises, some published and others left in manuscript, from Katherine Sutton (fl.1630-1663) and Agnes Beaumont (fl.1652-1720) to Anne Steele, Maria de Fleury (fl.1773-1791), Elizabeth Coltman (1761-1838), Henrietta Neale (1752-1802), and Maria Grace Saffery (1772-1858). Only when this tradition has been fully explored will the work of Baptist women in the long eighteenth century be correctly understood and their debt to Anne Dutton rightfully acknowledged.

The fall and rise of Benjamin Dutton: An early evangelical narrative of conversion and holiness

Matthew D. Haste

Matthew D. Haste is an Associate Professor of Biblical Spirituality and Biblical Counseling and Director of Professional Doctoral Studies at The Southern Baptist Theological Seminary.

In late October 1747, George Whitefield (1714–1770) worked through a stack of overdue correspondence in a small town outside of Charleston, South Carolina. Though weary from his recent trip down the east coast, he took time to pen a moving letter to a woman in a distant English village, reporting the tragic news that her husband had perished at sea. The well-known evangelist wanted to comfort her with a personal visit, as he had been a guest in her home before, but he entrusted her to God. "This is indeed a heavy stroke," he wrote, "But omnipotence can enable you to bear it. Now is the time to prove the strength of Jesus Christ."[1] Whitefield went on to assure the woman that her husband had died in the Lord: "Your husband was the Lord's servant. No doubt he is at rest. I heard him pray a little before he embarked. Weep not for him too much, nor for yourself."[2] The recipient of this unpublished letter is more familiar to historians than its subject.

Anne Dutton (1692–1765) was the most prolific female Baptist author of the eighteenth century.[3] She wrote over fifty works, published hundreds of letters, and

---

1 Letter of condolence from George Whitefield to Mrs. Anne Dutton, October 29, 1747, Huntingdonshire Archives, UK. Whitefield's letter informing Anne of Benjamin's death is included with the will of Benjamin Dutton. Anne's report of receiving this news can be found in Anne Dutton, "Letter XXXVI," in *Letters*, 1:179–80.

2 Letter of condolence from Whitefield to Dutton. Whitefield generously closed the letter as follows: "I can only say that if our Lord brings me to England next year, you shall be heartily welcome to live with me. My dear yokefellow joins most cordially in this invitation. I hope you will accept it."

3 The majority of Dutton's works are now available in a seven-volume set edited by JoAnn Ford Watson, entitled *Selected Spiritual Writings of Anne Dutton: Eighteenth-Century, British-Baptist, Woman Theologian* (Macon, GA: Mercer University Press, 2003–2015). She is variously recognized as having published more individual works than any other Baptist woman in the eighteenth century. Timothy Whelan considers her "among the most published nonconformist women writ-

was recognized on both sides of the Atlantic for her religious zeal and spiritual wisdom.[4] Her early associations with high Calvinism and her correspondence with evangelical luminaries such as Howell Harris (1714–1773), Selena Hastings (1707–1791), John Wesley (1703–1791), and Whitefield, have long attracted the interest of scholars.[5] By contrast, her husband Benjamin (1691–1747) is relatively unknown.[6] This article aims to address this lacuna.

To be sure, Benjamin's contributions to the Revival were comparatively modest. Yet, his pastorate at Great Gransden in Huntingdonshire was fruitful, at a time when much of the Baptist work in England was languishing. While many Baptists were skeptical of the Revival, Benjamin traveled to Wales to partner with Harris and opened his pulpit to Whitefield. The following year, he journeyed to America, where he made acquaintance with Thomas Prince, Sr. (1687–1758) and preached throughout Northeast England. Most significantly, Benjamin penned a spiritual

---

ers of the seventeenth and eighteenth centuries" (Timothy Whelan, *Other British Voices: Women, Poetry, and Religion, 1766–1840* [New York: Palgrave Macmillan, 2015], 14).

4 The key biographical studies on Dutton are as follows: Michael A.G. Haykin, *8 Women of Faith* (Wheaton, IL: Crossway, 2016), 53–65; idem, *A Cloud of Witness: Calvinistic Baptists in the 18th Century* (Darlington, England: Evangelical Times, 2006), 33–38; Joseph Ivimey, *A History of the English Baptists: Comprising the Principal Events of the History of the Protestant Dissenters, During the Reign of George III. And of the Baptist Churches in London, with Notices of Many of the Principal Churches in the Country during the Same Period* (London: Isaac Taylor Hinton; Holdsworth & Ball, 1830), 4:509–10; Michael D. Sciretti, Jr., "'Feed My Lambs': The Spiritual Direction Ministry of Calvinistic British Baptist Anne Dutton During the Early Years of the Evangelical Revival" (PhD diss., Baylor University, 2009); Stephen J. Stein, "A Note on Anne Dutton, Eighteenth-Century Evangelical," *Church History* 44 (1975): 485–491; H.G. Tibbutt, "Mrs. Dutton's Husband," *Bedfordshire Biographies* 38 (Autumn 1965): 65–67; JoAnn Ford Watson, "Introduction," in *Selected Spiritual Writings of Anne Dutton: Eighteenth-Century, British-Baptist, Woman Theologian*, vol. 1, *Letters*, ed. Watson (Macon, GA: Mercer University Press, 2003), xi–lii; Whitebrook, "Mrs. Ann Dutton," 129–146; Huafang Xu, "Anne Dutton (1692–1765)," in *The British Particular Baptists*, ed. Michael A.G. Haykin (Springfield, MO: Particular Baptist Press, 2018), 4:106. Sciretti's historiography provides a helpful overview of how Anne's legacy has been variously interpreted. See Sciretti, "Feed My Lambs," 8–17. See also my work on Dutton in Matthew D. Haste, *Helped on Our Way to Heaven: Eighteenth-Century English Baptists on Marriage* (Eugene, OR: Pickwick, 2023).

5 Sciretti's work on Dutton is the most extensive to date and includes a thorough historiographical sketch. Sciretti, "Feed My Lambs," 8–17. Peter Toon defined hyper-Calvinism as a system of belief that emphasized "the immanent acts of God—eternal justification, eternal adoption, and the eternal covenant of grace as the grounds for salvation" at the expense of "minimising the moral and spiritual responsibility of sinners to God." As a young woman, Anne was exposed to Hyper-Calvinism through the writings of Joseph Hussey (1660–1726) and the ministry of her London pastor, John Skepp (1675–1721). Skepp is often recognized as a conduit of Hyper-Calvinism into Particular Baptist churches due to influence on John Gill (1697–1771), John Brine (1703–1765), and Anne Dutton. His only published work was printed posthumously: *Divine Energy; or The Efficacious Operations of the Spirit of God upon the Soul of Man* (1722). He pastored the Cripplegate church in London from 1710 until his death in 1721. For the larger context of this controversy, see Peter Toon, *The Emergence of Hyper-Calvinism in English Nonconformity 1689–1765* (London: Olive Tree, 1967), 74–85; Geoffrey F. Nuttall, "Northamptonshire and *The Modern Question*: A Turning-Point in Eighteenth-Century Dissent," *Journal of Theological Studies* NS 16 (1965): 101–23. The extent to which hyper-Calvinism shaped Dutton's theology has been overstated by scholars who have failed to consider the full corpus of her writings and her later participation in the Evangelical Revival.

6 The principle primary sources for Benjamin are his and Anne's respective autobiographies: Anne Dutton, *A Brief Account of the Gracious Dealings of God, with a Poor, Sinful, Unworthy Creature, in Three Parts*, in *Selected Spiritual Writings of Anne Dutton: Eighteenth-Century, British-Baptist, Woman Theologian*, vol. 3, *Autobiography*, ed. JoAnn Ford Watson (Macon, GA: Mercer University Press, 2006), 1–251; and Benjamin Dutton, *The Superaboundings of the Exceeding Riches of God's Free Grace towards the Chief of the Chief of Sinners* (London: J. Hart, 1743).

autobiography that candidly addressed his post-conversion struggles with alcohol. This work provides a fascinating window into one early evangelical's pursuit of practical holiness.

While Benjamin is typically a tangential subject in the few studies that reference him, he left behind a unique artifact of early eighteenth-century piety that is worthy of exploration. This article will therefore examine the work with a particular focus on his conversion, his pursuit of practical holiness, and his decades-long struggle with alcohol. The following sketch of his life and ministry is constructed from the details available in his and his wife's respective autobiographies as well as various archival material.

The Life and Ministry of Benjamin Dutton
Benjamin was the youngest of six children born to Matthew Dutton (d. 1719), who pastored a Dissenting congregation in Bedfordshire, and his wife (née Brown), who lived to age ninety-two. As an adult, Benjamin reflected on his childhood with appreciation, as he remembered the stability of his parents' marriage and his father's consistent concern for his soul.[7]

Despite the efforts of his pious parents, Benjamin considered himself a proud child, though various trials occasionally motivated brief periods of strict living.[8] A near-death experience at age thirteen prompted great soul-searching, but not yet conversion: "I looked for strength in myself, and knew not what it was to trust in the strength of Christ."[9] Soon after this incident, Benjamin was apprenticed to a clothier at Newbury, where he boarded with a Presbyterian couple. In these years, the young man dedicated himself to learning his trade and dreaming of future wealth. In retrospect, he recognized a growing pride and vanity that caused his heart to grow cold to God and resulted in his first incident with drunkenness.[10] His "love of ale" would plague him for years to come.[11]

Nonetheless, Benjamin soon experienced a deep stirring of conviction that resulted in his conversion.[12] He began meeting weekly with a group of young men to study theology and pray together. This group is noteworthy for the role it played in Benjamin's budding spirituality and also for the glimpse it provides into a pre-

---

[7] His father was a significant spiritual influence throughout his life. Benjamin sought advice from his father into adulthood and his father encouraged him during his various struggles. Dutton, *Superaboundings of the Exceeding Riches of God's Free-Grace*, 127–28.

[8] For example, see Dutton, *Superaboundings of the Exceeding Riches of God's Free-Grace*, 19.

[9] Dutton, *Superaboundings of the Exceeding Riches of God's Free-Grace*, 25.

[10] He noted, "Thus, I idolized myself, and my imagined beauty and took great delight in viewing myself in the glass, and thinking myself so handsome, that everybody almost could not but fall in love with me" (Dutton, *Superaboundings of the Exceeding Riches of God's Free-Grace*, 28).

[11] Dutton, *Superaboundings of the Exceeding Riches of God's Free-Grace*, 30.

[12] Dutton, *Superaboundings of the Exceeding Riches of God's Free-Grace*, 31.

Revival religious society devoted to the pursuit of personal piety.[13] Benjamin was soon baptized into membership of a local Presbyterian congregation pastored by James Peirce (1674–1726), who would later gain infamy for his role in the Salters' Hall Controversy of 1719.[14] As a young believer, Benjamin wrestled with important theological questions, demonstrating a commitment to anchor his doctrine in Scripture.[15] After his father made financial arrangements to fulfill his commitment as an apprentice, he began formal training for ministry, first under Isaac Robinson (d. 1723) at Chesham, and later under the Independent minister John Magee (d. 1743) at Ravenstonedale, Cumbria, then in London and later Glasgow.[16] In these years, Benjamin declined several opportunities to preach, believing that he should wait until he finished his studies—a decision he would later regret.[17]

Early years of ministry
After his father's death in August of 1719, Benjamin moved to Northampton to study under John Moore (1662–1726), pastor of the Baptist Church at College Lane.[18] This community, or perhaps even this pastor, eventually acquainted him

---

13 According to Benjamin, there were sixteen young men in this group, which met early on the Lord's Day each week. In their meetings, they prayed together, read aloud from various theological works, and shared the concerns of their souls. Benjamin noted that they regularly read from the *Westminster Shorter Catechism* (1647), Thomas Vincent's *The Shorter Catechism Explained* (1674), Matthew Henry's *Exposition of the Five Books of Moses* (1707), and John Wilkin's *A Discourse Concerning the Gift of Prayer* (1651). Dutton, *Superaboundings of the Exceeding Riches of God's Free-Grace*, 69.

14 Benjamin first began attending this church at the request of his master and joined despite his theological scruples with Peirce, owing in large part to his relationship with the aforementioned young men who attended there. Benjamin noted that Peirce "seemed then to be a Baxterian, but for aught we knew was clear in the Doctrine of the Trinity" (Dutton, *Superaboundings of the Exceeding Riches of God's Free-Grace*, 26). Peirce's congregation at Newbury was large enough to fund an assistant, though Benjamin was unimpressed with the preaching of either man. After Benjamin left the church at the conclusion of his apprenticeship, Peirce later moved to Exeter, where his orthodoxy on the Trinity was called into question. For more on Peirce and the Salters' Hall Controversy, including a careful examination of Peirce's theology, see Jesse Franklin Owens, "The Salters' Hall Controversy of 1719" (PhD diss., The Southern Baptist Theological Seminary, 2021).

15 By the end of this period, Benjamin was decidedly committed to a Calvinistic understanding of the doctrines of grace: "Hence, was I led to see, that absolute election, particular redemption, effectual calling, free justification, final perseverance, and eternal glorification, all joined together as links in a chain; so that where the one is, the other is and shall be" (Dutton, *Superaboundings of the Exceeding Riches of God's Free-Grace*, 73). The "links in a chain" imagery traced back to William Perkins' famous work *A Golden Chain*, first published in 1591.

16 Isaac Robinson pastored a Presbyterian church in Chesham, Buckinghamshire, where Benjamin first studied. Benjamin was given opportunities to teach at Chesham, but he declined requests to preach until he had completed his studies. For more on Robinson, see W.H. Summers, *History of the Congregational Churches in the Berks, South Oxon, and South Bucks Association, with Notes on the Earlier Nonconformist History of the District* (Newbury, England: W. J. Blacket, 1905), 39. For more on Magee, see Alx. Gordon, "John Magee: A Venturesome Divine," *Transactions of the Congregationalist Historical Society* 7 (1916): 200–12. Dutton gives no explanation for why he moved about during his years of studies, but his enrolment in Glasgow was due to dissenters being barred from English universities at the time. Dutton, *Superaboundings of the Exceeding Riches of God's Free-Grace*, 69.

17 Dutton, *Superaboundings of the Exceeding Riches of God's Free-Grace*, 75.

18 Moore became the pastor of this fledgling church in 1700 and, though baptistic himself, he led the church to formalize its established practice of mixed communion. The church added 264 members during his 25 years of labor. Moore's twenty-five-year ministry at College Street, including his ignominious end, is summarized in Taylor, *History of College Street*, 4–14. Moore was remembered by Taylor as "the first great pastor of College Street," though his tenure would eventually end

with a young widow named Anne, whose first husband had died in the early years of their marriage.[19] Years later, Benjamin recounted his first impressions of her:

> In the twenty-eighth year of my age, the Lord was graciously pleased to give me a very suitable yokefellow, a daughter of Abraham indeed, one of great faith and light in the Gospel. The first time I was in her company with other friends, I was much taken with her Christian discourse, and had this thought passed through my mind, that she would make a brave minister's wife.[20]

Anne's announcement of this change in her life was less descriptive. She noted only, "After I had been at Northampton some time, I was again married."[21] The two wed sometime in 1720 and settled in Northampton.

Soon after, Benjamin joined a nearby church that affirmed his call to ministry "after trial of [his] gifts unto satisfaction."[22] Benjamin did not name this church but it may have been the Strict Baptist congregation that met in a private home in these years and later built a meeting house known as the Chapel on the Green.[23] Based on the passing references to this church in her autobiography, it appears that Anne

---

in sorrow and scandal. At some point after Anne moved to London with her first husband, Moore fell into sin that spelled disaster for him and the church. Despite his repentance, the church declined considerably. As Taylor commented, "'He died with grief' is the brief and eloquently pathetic statement in the Church Book" marking the end of his life in January, 1726 (Taylor, *History of College Street*, 13). For a more extensive history, see John Taylor, *Bi-Centenary Volume. History of College Street Church, Northampton, with Biographies of Pastors, Missionaries, and Preachers; and Notes of Sunday Schools, Branch Churches, and Workers, Illustrated with Portraits and Drawings* (Northampton: Taylor & Son, Dryden, 1897).

19 Little is known about Anne's first husband, to the extent that there is some disagreement about his name. According to public records in Northampton recovered by Sciretti, Anne Williams married Thomas Cattell on January 4, 1715. He died in 1719 or 1720 for unknown reasons.

20 Dutton, *Superaboundings of the Exceeding Riches of God's Free-Grace*, 129.

21 Dutton, *A Brief Account*, 3:65. Anne addressed the issue of choosing a spouse in a letter to a young man, encouraging him to only marry in the Lord: "Choose such a one for your Companion, that loves Christ, and is of the same Mind with you, for entertaining of his Servants, attending on his Service, and for the Advancement of his Honour and Interest in the Earth; or your Settling for these Ends, will be in vain" (Anne Dutton, "Letter XXXIV," in *Letters on Spiritual Subjects, and Divers Occasions; Sent to Relations and Friends*, in *Selected Spiritual Writings of Anne Dutton: Eighteenth-Century, British-Baptist, Woman Theologian*, vol. 5, *Miscellaneous Correspondence*, ed. JoAnn Ford Watson [Macon, GA: Mercer University Press, 2007], 169).

22 Dutton, *Superaboundings of the Exceeding Riches of God's Free-Grace*, 129.

23 This church was formed around 1700 by a group of Northampton members who belonged to the Strict Baptist congregation in Stevington, Bedfordshire pastored by Daniel Negus. For more on the Stevington church, which had some ties to John Bunyan (1628–1688), see George E. Page, "Baptist Churches in the Bedford Area," *Baptist Quarterly* 14 (1952): 358–60. According to Taylor, this group first met in a barn at St. James' End. By 1724, near the time when Benjamin Dutton may have been a member, they were meeting in the home of Edward Garner in Quart Pot Lane. In 1732, they called John Moore's son-in-law, Charles Rogers (d. 1782), as their pastor after the latter disputed with the College Lane Church over their communion practices. This episode and the preceding details are recorded at length in Taylor, *History of College Street Church*, 15–19. After a series of pastors, the last of whom was installed in a service presided over by both Gill and Brine, the church known as the Chapel on the Green died out by mid-century and sold their building to the local Methodists. Evidencing his own possible relationship to the church, when Benjamin later led his Gransden congregation toward formalized Strict Baptist principles, he invited Rogers to preach on the occasion. See Nuttall, "Northamptonshire and *The Modern Question*," 120.

did not join her husband there.[24]

In the next five years, the couple would move multiple times as Benjamin pursued different short-term ministry opportunities throughout the Midlands and as far away as the Fens.[25] While his portrayal of this season is largely positive, it was a difficult time for Anne, both physically and spiritually.[26] Eventually, they settled in Wellingborough, where Benjamin continued to preach abroad.[27]

---

24 Anne mentioned Benjamin's call to ministry in the context of describing the circumstances that led them to Great Gransden. After reciting some of the details of Benjamin's early years, she explained, "After we were marry'd, for our present subsistence, he did something at his trade . . . [and] it was some time e'er the desire of his heart was given him, in his being statedly employ'd in the work of the ministry. But having been call'd to the work, by a church to which he join'd, he preach'd occasionally for a while at several places" (Dutton, *A Brief Account*, 3:141–2).

25 Their first stop was Wellingborough, where Anne enjoyed the preaching ministry of William Grant (d. 1771) and Benjamin began to preach occasionally in various churches in the area. Sciretti dates this move to the year 1725 based on a comment in one of Anne's letter (Sciretti, "Feed My Lambs," 87). Grant was trained in ministry under Richard Davis (1658–1714) of Rothwell, whose congregation planted the Wellingborough church in 1691. Grant was commissioned to Wellingborough in 1723 and would remain at this post until his death. According to one historian, he "laboured in the word and doctrine among the people forty-eight years, with great piety, cheerfulness, acceptance, and usefulness" (John Cole, *The History and Antiquities of Wellingborough, in the County of Northampton* [Northampton: Taylor & Son, 1865], 53). After hearing Grant preach, John Newton remarked, "A more excellent sermon I never heard, never was my heart so melted down since the golden days when I first attended Mr. Brewer and Mr. Whitefield" (Cited in Geoffrey Nuttall, "Baptists and Independents in Olney to the Time of John Newton," *Baptist Quarterly* 30 [January 1983]: 28–31). For more on the Wellingborough church, see Cole, *The History and Antiquities of Wellingborough*, 49–53. For more on Richard Davis, see David L. Wykes, "Davis, Richard (1617/18–1693x1700)," in *Oxford Dictionary of National Biography*, ed. H.C.G. Matthew and Brian Harrison (Oxford: Oxford University Press, 2004), 15:462–64.

26 Anne despised their time in Cambridgeshire, where Benjamin preached for over two years at Whittlesey and Wisbech, describing it as her personal captivity and exchanging frustrated correspondence with Grant about how forsaken she felt. Her letters to Grant are reproduced in Dutton, *A Brief Account*, 110–20, 122–26. She fell so ill at Whittlesey that she began to choose the passage she would wish to be preached at her funeral (Rev 7:16–17). Her record of this sickness can be found in Dutton, *A Brief Account*, 3:126–31. Benjamin, by contrast, reflected on these years with gratitude. Dutton, *Superaboundings of the Exceeding Riches of God's Free-Grace*, 130.

Little is known about the Baptist work at Whittlesey in these years, but *The Evans List* records an Anabaptist named Thomas Speechley pastoring a congregation there in 1715 (Cited in T.D. Atkinson, Ethel M. Hampson, E.T. Long, C.A.F. Meekings, Edward Miller, H.B. Wells and G.M.G. Woodgate, "Wisbech: Protestant Nonconformity," in *A History of the County of Cambridge and the Isle of Ely*, vol. 4, *City of Ely; Ely, N. and S. Witchford and Wisbech Hundreds*, ed. R.B. Pugh [London: Victoria County History, 2002], 250–51). The Wisbech congregation was likely the Particular Baptist church that met at Dead-Man's Lane in Wisbech led by its aged founding pastor William Rix (1642–1728). See Neil Walker and Thomas Craddock, *The History of Wisbech and the Fens* (Wisbech: Richard Walker, 1849), 394–96; Ivimey, *History of the English Baptists*, 4:459–60. Both congregations may have owed their origins to the ministry of David Culy (d. 1725), who was at one time associated with Davis' Rothwell congregation. On Culy, see "Culy, David (d. 1725)," in *Oxford Dictionary of National Biography*, 14:613. Whitebrook also references a sermon Benjamin preached at Cambridge in 1725 on John 16:27, Ps 31:99, and Prov 18:24. See Whitebrook, "Mrs. Ann Dutton," 134.

27 Often his preaching took him "pretty far distant from the place of our abode" as he reckoned. Dutton, *Superaboundings of the Exceeding Riches of God's Free-Grace*, 131. Anne interpreted the return to Wellingborough (and Grant's ministry) as the Lord's deliverance. Dutton, *A Brief Account*, 3:131. Benjamin recorded the same details with a decidedly different tone, "But as it was a fenny country, the air did not suit my wife's constitution, she being a weakly person; but brought on her such great illness, that obliged us to return to Wellingborough" (Dutton, *Superaboundings of the Exceeding Riches of God's Free-Grace*, 130). The Fens, as the region around Whittlesey is known, remain naturally marshy to this day and could indeed have been detrimental to Anne's health. The difficulties of this rugged landscape are sometimes credited for instilling tenacity in Andrew Fuller, who was born and raised in nearby Soham. See Peter Morden, *The Life and Thought of Andrew Fuller (1754–1815)* (Milton Keynes, England: Paternoster, 2015), 13–14.

Of note, he assisted the aged Baptist minister Benjamin Winckles (d. 1732) in Leicestershire for nearly three years.[28] The Arnesby Church minute book records several entries related to Benjamin in the years 1729–1731, revealing some of the tumultuous details of his time there. In July 1729, he was "cleared" from an unspecified accusation made by a fellow member named Joseph Horton. This episode may relate to what Benjamin described in his autobiography around this same time: "Many rose up against me in a merciless, hard-hearted, unforgiving Spirit, contemning and trampling me, as a poor helpless Worm under their Feet."[29] A year later, the record includes the following somber report: "Benjamin Dutton was cut off from the church for his great crimes though he did show his sorrow."[30] Though not mentioned explicitly, his excommunication was undoubtedly related to his ongoing struggles with drunkenness. Finally, in December of either 1730 or 1731, a blotted entry on a torn page of the book notes the following: "Benjamin Dutton ... his repentance for his evils ... church and was approved . . . received into the church." Though critical details are unavailable, it seems that the church accepted Benjamin's repentance for his repeated drunkenness, and he was restored into fellowship.[31] In his autobiography, Benjamin recorded his decision to swear off alcohol once and for all in detail.

Around the same time, Winckles and several men from the Arnesby church penned a letter affirming Benjamin's repentance and certifying his "usefulness in the Lord's work," which he included in his autobiography.[32] This statement of reference, which may have been occasioned by a new ministry opportunity at Great Gransden, included the signature of Joseph Horton, the very church member who had brought unknown charges against him in 1729.[33]

---

28 Dutton, *Superaboundings of the Exceeding Riches of God's Free-Grace*, 131. Benjamin Winckles pastored the Particular Baptist church at Arnesby for over 36 years, during which time the church grew by nearly 120 individuals, many of whom travelled significant distances for Sunday worship. The church entered a period of decline after Winckles' death before being revitalized under the ministry of Robert Hall, Sr. (1728–1791). For more on the history of the church, see Richard Hunt, "Record and Representation: The Minute Book of the Arnesby Particular Baptist Church," *Transactions of the Leicestershire Archaeological and Historical Society* 84 (2010): 151–63.

29 Dutton, *Superaboundings of the Exceeding Riches of God's Free-Grace*, 99.

30 The Arnesby Baptist Church minute book is housed in manuscript form in the Record Office for Leicestershire, Leicester, and Rutland, UK. For other disciplinary matters recorded by the church, see Hunt, "Record and Representation," 157–58.

31 The date of this entry coincides with the letter from Arnesby that Benjamin included in his autobiography (Dutton, *Superaboundings of the Exceeding Riches of God's Free-Grace*, 103).

32 Dutton, *Superaboundings of the Exceeding Riches of God's Free-Grace*, 103. As to the date, in both the Arnesby Church minute book and *Superaboundings*, the date is listed as December 1730/1731 for reasons that are unclear.

33 Anne does not seem to have engaged in the work at Arnesby, but moved her membership from the Cripplegate congregation in London to Grant's church in Wellingborough during these years. Dutton, *A Brief Account*, 3:134. She commented, "And thus, [Benjamin] preach'd during great part of the time of our last abode at Wellingborough, which was about three years, at several places, some of which were pretty far distant" (Dutton, *A Brief Account*, 3:142).

Ministry at Gransden and beyond

Though Great Gransden was a mere fifteen miles from where Benjamin was born, he had never heard of it when he was first invited to preach there in 1730.[34] The church was started in 1694 by local members of a nearby congregation who had formerly traveled to sit under the ministry of Francis Holcroft (d. 1692). Two years after Holcroft's death, individuals from that congregation living in Gransden and Croydon began meeting together, often alternating locations between the two villages. When Benjamin was formally installed as pastor in 1732, the church had been without a consistent pastor for nearly five years.[35]

Anne was initially hesitant about the Gransden opportunity, but in time, concluded it was from the Lord as she reached a "holy resignation" to embark on the work while meditating on Jesus' command to Peter to "feed my lambs" (John 21:15).[36] In Anne's words, she chose to pursue God's "glorious service, something to *do for* him."[37] Benjamin recorded this conclusion with unmistakable joy: "As for my wife, she loved the people, though she never saw them, and had several words from the Lord to encourage her to come."[38] The couple moved to Great Gransden in June 1731 and Benjamin was installed as pastor there the following October.

The Duttons had weathered various trials in their first decade of marriage, including spiritual difficulties, health issues, Benjamin's struggles with alcohol, and Anne's discontent over their circumstances. In contrast, their years at Great Gransden proved fruitful for both husband and wife.[39] The church grew under Benjamin's leadership, necessitating the construction of a new meetinghouse that is still standing in the village today.[40] According to the nineteenth-century historian Joseph Ivimey (1773–1834), the church expanded to fifty members with some two

---

34 Dutton, *Superaboundings of the Exceeding Riches of God's Free-Grace*, 131.

35 Under Benjamin's leadership, the two congregations consolidated into a Particular Baptist church at Great Gransden in 1733. For more on Holcroft, see A.C.B., "Holcroft, Francis (1629?–1693)," in *Dictionary of National Biography*, ed. Sydney Lee (London: Smith, Elder, & Co., 1891), 27:15.

36 Dutton, *A Brief Account*, 3:143–45. Michael Sciretti identifies the call to Gransden as the climax of the second part of her autobiography, noting that Anne "soon came to believe that everything that transpired over the previous decade was a great preparation for the work of her life in this small Huntingdonshire town" (Sciretti, "Feed My Lambs," 93).

37 Dutton, *A Brief Account*, 3:150. In this resignation, Sciretti argues that Anne reached "the heights of a *Calvinist* mysticism*," where "the highest rungs of the ladder to God is willing and living service, *soli Deo gloria*" (Sciretti, "Feed My Lambs," 98).

38 Dutton, *Superaboundings of the Exceeding Riches of God's Free-Grace*, 132. When a subsequent opportunity emerged that would have taken them to London instead, Benjamin marveled at Anne's resolve, "My Wife's heart was not at all inclin'd to go thither, but cleave to *Gransden* people" (Dutton, *Superaboundings of the Exceeding Riches of God's Free-Grace*, 132). Sciretti correctly points out Wheeler Robinson's flawed conclusions about Anne's unwillingness to go to Gransden (Sciretti, "Feed my Lambs," 99).

39 Dutton, *A Brief Account*, 3:154–56.

40 Benjamin recounts the details of his fundraising efforts for the new meeting house in Dutton, *Superaboundings of the Exceeding Riches of God's Free-Grace*, 135–43. This section of his autobiography serves as a polemic for his financial integrity in the process.

Though living an ocean apart in these years, Benjamin and Anne each continued to make meaningful contributions to the Evangelical Revival taking place on both sides of the Atlantic. Of course, neither could know that Benjamin would soon meet his end in those very waters.

After receiving news of her husband's death from Whitefield, Anne wrote to her brother, reflecting on both the weight of this loss and the Lord's mercy in her suffering. She reflected, "This stroke, my brother, is so great that it almost overcomes my weak nature. But, glory to my God, I feel the everlasting arms underneath me, and, when ready to faint, my dear Lord gives me a cordial."[49] In her autobiography, she expanded on her sorrow at the news: "How grieving was this to my nature! How trying to my faith and hope! The real loss of my dear yokefellow, the seeming denial of my earnest prayers, and the failure of my expectation, as to his return, which I hoped might have been included in God's never-failing promises, with the distress of the church, occasion'd thereby, came upon me all at once."[50] Benjamin Dutton left behind a grieving widow and a distressed church, but his untimely death did not rob future generations of learning from his life. The following section will analyze his conversion and battle with alcohol, while situating his spirituality in its larger historical context.

Analysis of Superaboundings

Benjamin's autobiography was a deliberate imitation of the more well-known work by John Bunyan (1628–1688), with an emphasis on his surpassing unworthiness. Whereas Bunyan wrote *Grace Abounding to the Chief of Sinners* in 1666, Benjamin titled his work *The Superaboundings of the Exceeding Riches of God's Free Grace towards the Chief of the Chief of Sinners* (1743).[51] He was one of many in this era who published his personal spiritual experiences in the form of the developing genre of conversion narrative.

The concept of a personal conversion narrative finds its theological roots in the Reformation, though few examples exist from that era. Bruce Hindmarsh summarized the historical phenomena that led to this development: "The Renaissance made people more aware of themselves as individuals, and the church made them more aware of themselves as sinners."[52] In subsequent generations, the English

---

little before he embarked" on the ship that foundered on its journey back to England (Letter of condolence from George Whitefield to Mrs. Anne Dutton, October 29, 1747, Huntingdonshire Archives, UK).

49 Dutton, "Letter XXXVI," 1:180. Anne also spoke of her husband's death in other correspondence. See Anne Dutton, "Letter XXVI" and "Letter LIII," in *Letters VIII*, in *Words of Grace*, 7:372-3, 424-6; Anne Dutton, "Letter LII," "Letter LIV," "Letter LVII," "Letter LX," and "Letter LXIII," in *Miscellaneous Correspondence*, 5:215-7, 220-1, 230-3, 238-9, 242-3.

50 Dutton, *A Brief Account*, 3:243.

51 The British historian H.G. Tibbutt noted the similarities between the two spiritual autobiographies some fifty years ago, but to date, no analysis has explored how Bunyan's work, or the tradition it represented, shaped Dutton's spirituality (Tibbutt, "Mrs. Dutton's Husband," 65).

52 Bruce Hindmarsh, *The Evangelical Conversion Narrative: Spiritual Autobiography in Early Modern England* (New York: Oxford Press, 2005), 32.

hundred to three hundred hearers.⁴¹ In addition to publishing his autobiography in 1743, Benjamin became a respected minister who was invited to preach in various parts of England, Wales, and eventually America. From Great Gransden, Anne published her first work in 1734 and by 1743 she had twenty-one works in print.⁴² She considered her books—which would come to number over fifty by the time of her death—her "children," a poignant image from the barren authoress.⁴³ These developments set the stage for Benjamin's fateful trip to the American colonies that ended in his untimely death. Determined to raise money for the church and to share Anne's writing with an American audience, Benjamin set sail in August 1743.

History has left little record of Benjamin's time in America. Based on Anne's references to their correspondence, it seems he was active in ministry, bearing spiritual fruit and accomplishing his purpose of raising funds for the Great Gransden meeting house.⁴⁴ His first stop may have been Boston, where he delivered various materials on behalf of the London publisher John Lewis (d. 1755) to Thomas Prince, Sr., the esteemed pastor of Old South Church.⁴⁵ Lewis, whose evangelical magazine helped expand Anne's influence, included a letter of introduction for Benjamin, whom he called "a faithful minister of Jesus Christ and an hearty friend to his cause."⁴⁶ Prince would note in a copy of one of Anne's works that her husband "came to New England and traveled and preached here."⁴⁷ At some point, Benjamin crossed paths with Whitefield, but little else has been discovered about his labors in America.⁴⁸

---

41 Ivimey, *History of the English Baptists*, 4:509. For an analysis of key passages in the Gransden church book, see H.G. Tibbutt, "Pattern of Change," *Transactions of the Congregational Historical Society* 20, no. 5 (May 1967): 170–73.

42 Anne listed her twenty-one published works at the conclusion of her biography published in 1743. Dutton, *A Brief Account*, 3:207–8.

43 Dutton, *A Brief Account*, 3:205.

44 Anne recorded, "His labours in the Gospel of Christ, were blest for the edification of the saints, and for the conversion of some sinners, not less than eleven or twelve souls" (Dutton, *A Brief Account*, 3:240). The money he raised was sent back to Gransden on a separate vessel.

45 Prince, from whom the city of Princeton, Massachusetts derived its name, was a well-respected pastor who supported Whitefield's efforts in New England and ministered in the region for over forty years. In his personal library, he possessed octavos of Anne's *A Letter to All the Saints on the General Duty of Love* (1743) and Benjamin's *Superaboundings*, as well as Anne's *A Brief Account* in duodecimo, which Benjamin likely gave him at this meeting. In one copy, he scribbled a note indicating that Benjamin travelled and preached in New England in the 1740s. See *The Prince Library. A Catalogue of the Collection of Books and Manuscripts which Formerly Belonged to the Reverend Thomas Prince* (Boston: Alfred Mudge & Son, 1870), 94. For more on Prince, see Clifford K. Shipton, *Sibley's Harvard Graduates* (Boston: Massachusetts Historical Society, 1937), 5:341–68.

46 John Lewis to Thomas Prince, Sr., August 20, 1743, Davis MSS, Massachusetts Historical Society, cited in Sciretti, "Feed My Lambs," 286. Lewis said of Anne, "I believe his wife is as eminent a saint, and as useful a member (in her sphere) in the Church-Militant, as any our Lord has. Her works shall witness. Her letters have been sweetly bless'd to my poor soul." In this letter, Lewis identifies Anne as the authoress behind the many letters in his magazine that were anonymously attributed to "A Friend in the Country."

47 *Prince Library*, 94.

48 In his unpublished letter to Anne informing her of Benjamin's death, Whitefield noted that he "heard him pray a

How then did Benjamin Dutton's spiritual memoir serve to establish his identity as an early evangelical? As he explained in the preface to *Superaboundings*, he had long desired to record a testimony of God's work in his life, but he was apprehensive to do so for various reasons. By 1743, Benjamin could speak openly of how God had not only redeemed him but also delivered him from great sin—particularly, the sin of drunkenness that figures prominently in his narrative. He self-consciously addressed fellow sinners with pastoral sensitivity: "This little piece is designed for the poor and needy, for humble, mourning souls, that are groaning under the power and prevalency of sin ... And who knows but the Lord may bless it unto some such, for the encouragement of their faith and hope in God, while I declare how He hath helped me, the chief of the chief of sinners!"[58]

It was common for spiritual autobiographies to serve a ministerial purpose, often through direct address to the reader and various instructive comments.[59] What distinguishes Dutton's work is the extensive focus on the temptations he faced *after* his conversion. The "help" he had received from God was not merely salvific but moved him towards practical holiness. Divine aid is central to Benjamin's understanding of his conversion, his perseverance through struggles with sin, and his eventual deliverance from the temptation to drink alcohol.

His conversion
Benjamin applied the "morphology of conversion" in the typical Puritan-evangelical pattern by recounting a period of conviction over sin, eventual comfort from the scriptures (Ps 51 and Isa 53, in particular), and a concluding joy in the provision of Christ as Savior. He was especially moved by the notion that Christ's death could be rightly applied to him personally: "How did, and how doth this sovereign grace, fill my poor soul with wonder, with joy unspeakable, and with love towards him who first loved me, and gave his only-begotten, his own, his dear Son for *me*, in *my* room and stead!"[60] He described his freedom and subsequent bliss in terms that echoed Bunyan: "And I had all my loads and burdens taken off me, and was like a person in another world for several days. I scarce knew, several times, where I was, or what I was about."[61] His newfound freedom produced sincere love for God, which he expressed in intimate terms.[62]

After this experience, Benjamin began to see spiritual growth in various areas

---

58 Dutton, *Superaboundings of the Exceeding Riches of God's Free-Grace*, vii.

59 In reflecting on his own childhood, he encouraged parents to teach their children according to the Scriptures because "God can by his Spirit ... impress his Word upon the hearts, even of little children" (Dutton, *Superaboundings of the Exceeding Riches of God's Free-Grace*, 18).

60 Dutton, *Superaboundings of the Exceeding Riches of God's Free-Grace*, 43–44.

61 Dutton, *Superaboundings of the Exceeding Riches of God's Free-Grace*, 46.

62 As proof, he cites a particular incident when he was so distracted by thoughts of Christ, that his mistress commented that he must be in love. "I was in love indeed," Benjamin noted, "But not in that way which she intended." According to Anne, he was around seventeen at this time (Dutton, *A Brief Account*, 3:141).

Puritan emphasis on introspection and experimental piety provided what Edmund Morgan termed the "morphology of conversion."[53] After the Act of Toleration expanded freedom for religious expression, this pattern was more frequently articulated in published narratives. Hindmarsh's extensive study of this literature has demonstrated that the form for conversion narratives was largely supplied by Calvinistic Puritans, with an emphasis on the pursuit of assurance within the theological matrix of law and gospel. Bunyan's *Grace Abounding* provided the essential outline, which included: (1) a reflection on pious childhood influences and early spiritual interests; (2) the individual's descent into worldliness and hardness of heart; (3) an initial experience of conviction that often led to self-exertion but not salvation; (4) despair over one's inability to attain righteousness through keeping the law; and finally, (5) the conversion climax, which produced joy in God, relief of the conscience, and freedom for service.

Jerald Brauer has argued that this same structure can be observed in both England and New England Puritanism and was retained during the first phase of the Revival.[54] This point illustrates the continuity between the Puritans and early evangelicals, particularly in relation to the Dissenters who ministered in England in the early decades of the eighteenth century. Scholars have often noted the lack of vitality among Dissenting churches prior to the Revival, but, as Geoffrey Nuttall has pointed out, there were some who were "Evangelical before the Revival."[55] In fact, in an article aimed at shedding light on this dark period of Dissenting history, Nuttall pointed to Benjamin Dutton's autobiography as an example of the sparks of intense devotion among Dissenters that scholars have sometimes overlooked.

While the recorded experiences of early evangelicals shared many similarities with the experimental piety of the Puritans, their narratives bore distinct marks of the early modern world. As Hindmarsh has described, unprecedented geographical movement and social dislocation meant that "religious experience became far more voluntary and self-conscious" in the eighteenth century, and as a result, "spiritual autobiography played a crucial role by allowing believers to negotiate an identity that could no longer be merely assumed."[56] Furthermore, for individuals like Dutton who grew up in the Dissenting tradition, in the home of a pious pastor no less, his conversion was "not *away* from his family of origin or community of faith, but *into* it more deeply."[57]

---

53 Edmund S. Morgan, *Visible Saints: The History of a Puritan Idea* (New York: University Press, 1963), 68–9.

54 Cited in Hindmarsh, *Evangelical Conversion Narrative*, 53.

55 See, for example, Raymond Brown, *The English Baptists of the 18th Century* (London: Baptist Historical Society, 1986). Nuttall's article in 1981 sought to correct the over-generalization among scholars at the time that "Dissent was arid and moribund" prior to the Evangelical Revival (Geoffrey Nuttall, "Methodism and the Older Dissent: Some Perspectives," *Journal of the United Reformed Church History Society* 2, no. 8 [1981]: 259–74).

56 Hindmarsh, *Evangelical Conversion Narrative*, 79.

57 Hindmarsh makes this comment in reference to Anne Dutton, who was also raised in the Dissenting tradition (Hindmarsh, *Evangelical Conversion Narrative*, 300).

of his life, including personal modesty, joy in God, love for the church, generosity to the poor, faithfulness in his work, willingness to make restitutions to those whom he wronged, and a deep concern for unbelieving sinners.[63] He observed so much transformation in his disposition, he considered it as if he "really had been two persons."[64] Now, he "beheld God in everything," recognizing both God's work in the world and the responsibility he bore to work on God's behalf. His zeal for God manifested in a love for Christ, his Word, and unconverted sinners.[65] Like many others in his day, Benjamin's conversion sparked a desire toward evangelical usefulness.

In a typical spiritual memoir in this period, the author would next describe his call into service and subsequent details of his ministry. Benjamin's narrative followed this pattern in general with one notable exception. For Benjamin, the true climax of his story was not his conversion, but his freedom from the overwhelming temptation to alcohol. Indeed, he considered himself the chief of sinners precisely because his sinful drinking continued for so long after his conversion.[66]

His struggles
The existential bliss he initially experienced after his conversion was disrupted by two overlapping challenges: a season of spiritual desertion that exacerbated his ongoing struggles with alcohol. "It was winter with my soul," Dutton reported in characteristically Puritan terms, as he noted how the Lord withdrew his "reviving, comforting, and strengthening influences."[67] Dutton's mature reflections on this season offered his reader a spiritual theology for such experiences:

> When the soul is new married unto Christ, the Lord is pleased to shed abroad his love in the heart by the Holy Ghost, and to fill it with joy and peace in believing. ... This is God's usual way at first. He graciously condescends to give the soul sensible enjoyments, as best suiting its infant-state, and the day of its espousals. But ordinarily, after a little time, the Lord is pleased to withhold sensible enjoyments from the soul, and to exercise it with various trials; in order to bring it to trust him in the dark, and to believe in hope ... But in this, as in other things, the Lord acts according to his sovereign good pleasure, as shall most conduce to his own glory, and the good of his creature,

---

[63] Dutton, *Superaboundings of the Exceeding Riches of God's Free-Grace*, 51–66. He concluded, "Thus, through grace, there was a wonderful change in me!" (Dutton, *Superaboundings of the Exceeding Riches of God's Free-Grace*, 58).

[64] Dutton, *Superaboundings of the Exceeding Riches of God's Free-Grace*, 54.

[65] Dutton, *Superaboundings of the Exceeding Riches of God's Free-Grace*, 63–67.

[66] Dutton, *Superaboundings of the Exceeding Riches of God's Free-Grace*, vi.

[67] Dutton, *Superaboundings of the Exceeding Riches of God's Free-Grace*, 75. For more on this concept in Puritan thought, see David Chou-Ming Wang, "The English Puritans and Spiritual Desertion: A Protestant Perspective on the Place of Spiritual Dryness in the Christian Life," *Journal of Spiritual Formation and Soul Care* 3.1 (2010): 42–65.

and to fit it for that service which he hath design'd it for.[68]

During this difficult season, Benjamin both questioned his salvation and sometimes drank excessively. Though his drunkenness was infrequent (sometimes less than once per year), he recounted, "Several times, it had very bad effects, and brought much dishonor unto the Lord, and such great distress upon my own soul, which none fully knows but God alone."[69] In retrospect, he recognized Satan's efforts to lead him into sin and to provoke him to despair, even to the point of considering taking his own life.[70] As we know from the Arnesby church book, his struggles at times led to public embarrassment.

During such lapses, Benjamin experienced consolation in various ways. He recounted, "The Lord did not suffer me to perish in these deeps … Sometimes sooner, sometimes longer, sometimes one way, and sometimes another; sometimes by a promise brought to my mind, sometimes by some providence, and sometimes by the Word preached."[71] This prolonged struggle with temptation yields several observations about the spirituality of Benjamin Dutton.

First, he was thoroughly committed to practical holiness, even though he was drawn away into drunkenness on occasion. Throughout the narrative, Benjamin never sought to justify or minimize his actions; he groaned over his sin and cried out to God for help. He eventually realized that total abstinence from alcohol was necessary, as he explained, "for God's glory and my good and comfort."[72] There was no hint of antinomianism in Dutton's practical theology. Instead, as he recalled, "In faith and hope, I was kept striving, using the means, and waiting upon the Lord, believing that deliverance would come in God's time."[73]

Second, Dutton looked to the Scriptures for strength and encouragement. Retrospectively, he could recount many biblical passages that comforted him during his struggles.[74] He found support for complete abstinence in the Nazirite vow of Numbers 6 and the examples of Samson (Judg 13:3–5), Jeremiah (Jer 35), and John the Baptist (Luke 1:15). In summary, Benjamin concluded, "Thus sweetly, by many Scriptures, did the Lord teach me my duty, and draw my heart to deny myself for Christ, and thus good I found it to do!"[75]

---

68 Dutton, *Superaboundings of the Exceeding Riches of God's Free-Grace*, 77. This paragraph reads like a classic Puritan description of the soul's winter. See, for example, Thomas Goodwin's *A Child of Light Walking in Darkness* (1636) and Joseph Symonds' *The Case and Cure of a Deserted Soule* (1639).

69 Dutton, *Superaboundings of the Exceeding Riches of God's Free-Grace*, 80.

70 Dutton, *Superaboundings of the Exceeding Riches of God's Free-Grace*, 82.

71 Dutton, *Superaboundings of the Exceeding Riches of God's Free-Grace*, 82.

72 Dutton, *Superaboundings of the Exceeding Riches of God's Free-Grace*, 95.

73 Dutton, *Superaboundings of the Exceeding Riches of God's Free-Grace*, 96.

74 Some of the particular passages referenced (listed in order of reference) include Micah 7:8–10; Ps 27:6; Luke 22:31–32; Rom 8:31; 2 Cor 7:11; 1 Cor 9:25; Eph 5:18; Acts 2; Song 5:1; Isa 25:6; and Lev 10–11.

75 Dutton, *Superaboundings of the Exceeding Riches of God's Free-Grace*, 119.

Third, he was willing to include others in his fight with personal sin. He sought the prayer and support of other believers and referenced several specific churches that were praying for him.[76] Benjamin reflected, "I am persuaded that the Lord has heard the prayers of many for me who are now in glory. And oh, how will they rejoice to see me brought thither!"[77] Curiously, Anne was never mentioned in the context of his battles with alcohol, even though these episodes extended through their first decade of marriage. One can assume Anne shared in Benjamin's sorrow and shame over his public embarrassments.[78] Though she was discrete about her husband's drinking problems in her own writing, Anne surely supported her husband in prayer and counsel.[79] In fact, some of her published works may provide a clue into how she might have privately encouraged him through these difficulties.[80]

Finally, it is notable how Benjamin ultimately rested his hope in the triune God: "The Lord, who is the Helper of the poor and needy, and of such that have no helper, He in whom the fatherless find mercy, even He was my Helper!"[81] Benjamin described the divine aid he received in robust, orthodox Trinitarian terms; it was none other than "the mighty Jehovah, Father, Son, and Spirit; the Father, with all his love, the Son, with all his grace and fullness, the Spirit, with all his graces and comforts," who eventually gave him the strength to swear off all forms of alcohol

---

[76] Dutton, *Superaboundings of the Exceeding Riches of God's Free-Grace*, 97. He noted, in particular, a Mr. Pumphret at Gravel-Lane, who "pray'd earnestly with tears that the Lord would remember that poor young man who was labouring under the power of sin, and deliver him, and make him useful in his day and generation." At least two pastors wrote letters of affirmation in support of Benjamin. The necessity of these letters and Benjamin's references to his detractors reveal that at least some of his drunken episodes led to public embarrassment (Dutton, *Superaboundings of the Exceeding Riches of God's Free-Grace*, 101).

[77] Dutton, *Superaboundings of the Exceeding Riches of God's Free-Grace*, 97. Dutton referenced his father in particular who "dy'd in the faith of [his son's] deliverance."

[78] Benjamin's sins were clearly public knowledge. He referenced various detractors who showed him no mercy and rose to "blast [him] and hinder [his] usefulness" (Dutton, *Superaboundings of the Exceeding Riches of God's Free-Grace*, 101).

[79] In an undated letter discussing sin and temptation, Anne makes a brief reference to "the Affliction that has attended my Yoke-fellow," but no further details are given. If this is a reference to Benjamin's problems with alcohol, it seems to be her only published reference to his struggles. See Anne Dutton, "Letter XV," in *Letters on Spiritual Subjects, and Divers Occasions; Sent to Relatives and Friends*, vol. 1, in *Words of Grace*, 7:155.

[80] In 1745, Anne published a lengthy letter on the Christian's battle with sin and temptation. This letter was originally addressed to William Collins and included his recommendation as a preface. See Anne Dutton, *A Letter on the Being and Working of Sin, In the Soul of a Justified Man, as consistent with his State of Justification in Christ, and Sanctification through Him: With the Nature of his Obedience, and of his Comfort, consider'd: As the one is from God, and the other to Him; notwithstanding his Corruptions may be great, and his Grace small in his own Sight*, in *Words of Grace*, 7:63–83. On Dutton's ministry to Collins, see Sciretti, "Feed My Lambs," 361–63.

[81] Dutton, *Superaboundings of the Exceeding Riches of God's Free-Grace*, 89. On one occasion, Benjamin recounted an evening alone with God in which he experienced "such joys, such delights, such a feast, that far surpasseth all the carnal delights that this world can afford. ... Surely," he concluded, "it was a sealing time!" (Dutton, *Superaboundings of the Exceeding Riches of God's Free-Grace*, 88) Though he does not elaborate, this language suggests that Benjamin followed his wife (and Thomas Goodwin) in interpreting Ephesians 1:13 as indicating that being "sealed with the Spirit" amounted to a post-conversion, transcendent experience of grace.

by the end of the 1720s.[82]

His deliverance

Benjamin compared his deliverance from the temptation of alcohol to Yahweh's liberation of his people from Egypt.[83] At this time, he believed the Lord drew near to him and set his heart against sin, particularly against the offence which had been his "great wound."[84] In his autobiography, he included two letters of attestation to his renewed commitment and commented on the efforts of several detractors who seemed to question his sincerity. Nonetheless, Benjamin resolved "to leave off all strong liquors entirely."[85]

Such a commitment to total abstinence would have been uncommon at the time. Benjamin lived in a day when beer was a daily drink for many, while porter—invented in London in the 1720s—and gin, imported from the Continent, were growing in popularity.[86] When the Swiss travel writer César-François de Saussure (1705–1783) visited London in 1726, he remarked, "Would you believe it, although water is to be had in abundance in London and of fairly good quality, absolutely none is drunk? The lower classes, even the paupers, do not know what it is to quench their thirst with water. In this country nothing but beer is drunk!"[87]

Like their Puritan predecessors, evangelical preachers like Whitefield denounced drunkenness in their sermons, but calling for total abstinence was less common.[88] Though the so-called "Gin Craze" would inspire legislative action by mid-century, the temperance movement was several decades away. Various church books from this era record instances of members being dismissed for persistent drunkenness, but John Gill's comments on Ephesians 5:18 are representative of the general attitude toward moderation.[89] As Gill noted, "Drinking wine for neces-

---

[82] Dutton, *Superaboundings of the Exceeding Riches of God's Free-Grace*, 126. Walter Overstow's letter describing God's work in Benjamin's life is dated November 1728 and the letter from Benjamin Winckles and several men at Arnesby certifying Benjamin's usefulness to the Lord was written in December 1730/1731. Overstow pastored an Independent congregation at Oundle in Northamptonshire and encouraged Benjamin on several occasions during his struggles (Dutton, *Superaboundings*, 99). For more on the church Overstow pastored, see Coleman, *Independent Churches in Northamptonshire*, 250–61.

[83] Dutton, *Superaboundings of the Exceeding Riches of God's Free-Grace*, 95. Utilizing a common convention of the day, Dutton often compared his own experiences to that of various biblical characters.

[84] Dutton, *Superaboundings of the Exceeding Riches of God's Free-Grace*, 103.

[85] Dutton, *Superaboundings of the Exceeding Riches of God's Free-Grace*, 109.

[86] For an overview of developing attitudes toward alcohol in this time period, see James Nicholls, *The Politics of Alcohol: A History of the Drink Question in England* (Manchester: University Press, 2009).

[87] César de Saussure, *Letters from London, 1725–1730*, trans. Paul Scott (Newnham, England: Adnax Publications, 2006), 95.

[88] For example, see George Whitefield, *The Heinous Sin of Drunkenness. A Sermon preached by George Whitefield, A.B. of Pembroke College, Oxford* (Philadelphia: Andrew and William Bradford, 1740).

[89] For several examples, see H.G. Tibbutt, *Some Early Nonconformist Church Books* (Bedford: Bedfordshire Historical Record Society, 1972), 15–16. Based on these references, it seems the general practice was to appoint members of the church

sary use ... honest delight and lawful pleasure" is not prohibited in scripture, but "excessive drinking of it, and this voluntary, and with design, and on purpose" is condemned.[90] Similarly, Wesley was nuanced in his comments about alcohol depending on the type of liquor in question, but he concluded, "The abstaining from wine ... Christianity does not require."[91]

Benjamin Dutton agreed with this statement in principle, but his own struggles led him to determine that total abstinence was necessary for him. "However it might be with others," he concluded, "Yet with respect to myself, knowing my own frailty, I saw that I ought in no wise to drink wine or strong liquors, of any sort, nor to touch or taste thereof, lest I should bring dishonour to God and hurt to myself and others."[92] In time, this commitment enabled him to move beyond his struggles with alcohol to focus his energies on ministry.

Thus, he concluded, "And now deliverance is accomplished, shall I not rejoice and give thanks?"[93] Benjamin concluded this section of his autobiography by quoting a hymn by Richard Davis (1658–1714), the well-known minister of Rothwell with whom he had several personal ties.[94] Two stanzas are worth quoting in full:

My Jesus, He is all to me
Whate'er my soul can crave;
A Fountain free is Christ to me,
That I no want can have,

In famine, he is food to me,
In thirst he's royal wine;
No want can be attending me,
Since Jesus, he is mine.[95]

Conclusion

---

to first investigate charges and then proceed with confronting the individual. Of note is the oft-expressed concern that a man's drunkenness could impoverish his family, leading to the neglect of his wife and children.

90 John Gill, *An Exposition of the New Testament* (1809; repr., Paris, AR: Baptist Standard Bearer, 2005), 9:102.

91 John Wesley, *The Works of John Wesley*, 3rd ed. (1872; repr., Grand Rapids: Baker, 2002), 7:489. For an overview of Wesley's thoughts on the subject, see Ivan Burnett Jr., "Methodist Origins: John Wesley and Alcohol," *Methodist History* 13, no. 4 (July 1975): 3–17.

92 Dutton, *Superaboundings of the Exceeding Riches of God's Free-Grace*, 109. By his own reckoning, Dutton kept this vow the rest of his life, with only one notable setback. Once when ill, he drank a little wine in hopes it would help, but soon realized that the mere taste restored his inclination toward greater drinking. Thus, he concluded, he must henceforth abstain entirely, except at the Lord's Table. He resigned, "And by the Lord's strength, I never will, on any occasion whatsoever; tho' I was to live to the age of Methuselah" (Dutton, *Superaboundings of the Exceeding Riches of God's Free-Grace*, 122).

93 Dutton, *Superaboundings of the Exceeding Riches of God's Free-Grace*, 124.

94 For more on Richard Davis, see David L. Wykes, "Davis, Richard (1617/18–1693x1700)," in *Oxford Dictionary of National Biography*, 15:462–64.

95 Dutton, *Superabounding of the Exceeding Riches of God's Free-Grace s*, 125–6.

Near the end of his autobiography, Benjamin imagined what his final moments in this world might be like someday: "I have several times thought that if I was dying, had my senses, and was able to speak to those about me (but how it will be then I know not), I would say, 'Behold now, a wonder of wonders! The greatest wonder of grace that ever was! Here is the greatest sinner that ever was going to Heaven!'"[96]

Benjamin Dutton was surely not the greatest sinner that ever was, but his spiritual autobiography is a helpful resource, nonetheless. As an historical artifact from the early years of the Evangelical Revival, it illustrates one man's pursuit of holiness amid the complexities of indwelling sin. Through the lens of practical theology, it demonstrates the difficulty of casting off bad habits formed through years of folly and adds important nuance to the common narrative that can suggest that the Christian's journey *ends* (rather than *begins*) at conversion.

It is worth noting in closing that there is a common theme in both Whitefield's letter to Anne Dutton and Benjamin's reflection on his own future death. Despite his struggles with sin, both were confident that heavenly glory awaited him, a sentiment his wife also shared.[97] Thus, Benjamin Dutton died with assurance that "He who began a good work in [him] would bring it to completion at the day of Jesus Christ" (Phil 1:6).

---

96 Dutton, *Superaboundings of the Exceeding Riches of God's Free-Grace*, 145.

97 Anne's reflections on his death demonstrate a similar confidence in his salvation and subsequent "safe arrival in glory" (see A. Dutton, "Letter XXXVI," 1:180).

A resurgence of Benjamin Beddome studies: A bibliographic essay[1]

Yuta Seki

Yuta Seki is the Senior Pastor of Maple Avenue Baptist Church in Georgetown, Ontario, and is currently pursuing doctoral studies (Doctor of Educational Ministry) at The Southern Baptist Theological Seminary, where his area of research is the life and thought of Benjamin Beddome.

While he was an admired and influential pastor in his own day and in the generations following his death, Benjamin Beddome (1717–1795) is an unknown and forgotten figure amongst evangelical pastors and Christians today. This is true even amongst those who belong to the same heritage as Beddome, namely, the Baptist tradition. That Beddome was appreciated even forty years after his death is evident in a passing comment made in an obituary printed in *The Baptist Magazine*. The memoir is of Boswell Beddome who was, according to the obituary, the "grandson of the Rev. Benjamin Beddome, whose sermons and hymns are still the admiration of the churches."[2] This sentiment is corroborated by Robert Hall, Jr. (1764–1831) who published a volume of Beddome's hymns two decades prior and wrote in the preface:

> Mr. Beddome was on many accounts an extraordinary person ... As a Preacher, he was universally admired for the piety and unction of his sentiments, the felicity of his arrangement, and the purity, force, and simplicity of his language; all which were recommended by a delivery perfectly natural and graceful ... As a religious Poet, his excellence has long been known and acknowledged in dissenting congregations, in consequence of several admirable compositions, inserted in some popular compilations.[3]

---

1 The idea for this articles comes, in part, from Nathan A. Finn, "The Renaissance in Andrew Fuller Studies: A Bibliographic Essay," *Southern Baptist Journal of Theology* 17.2 (2013): 44–61.

2 "Memoir of the Late Mr. Boswell Beddome, of Weymouth," *Baptist Magazine* 27 (March 1835): 77.

3 Robert Hall, Jr., ed., "Recommendatory Preface," in Benjamin Beddome, *Hymns Adapted to Public Worship, or Family*

Benjamin Beddome served as the pastor of the Baptist church in Bourton-on-the-Water in the rural Cotswolds area in south central England for fifty-five years (1740–1795). He was beloved by the church in Bourton and his ministry was accepted by the broader English Particular Baptist community, and particularly by the Midland Association.[4] An example of such influence is seen in the use of Beddome's catechism, both in English Particular Baptist churches and at their training center, the Bristol Baptist Academy.[5] Though Beddome had invitations to minister in the more influential cities of Bristol and London, he chose to remain in the less visible town of Bourton-on-the-Water.[6] In terms of his placement in history, Michael A.G. Haykin wrote that Beddome ministered "between the times—those of Baptist advance in the seventeenth century and those of revival in the final decades of the eighteenth century."[7] Thus, he ministered in an obscure place and did not experience the extraordinary visible fruitfulness of his Baptist forebearers or posterity; yet, he was a useful pastor.

Beddome has much to teach the contemporary church, and his preaching, hymnody, and catechism are a good example of the richness of the Baptist tradition. While many of his works are extant, research on Beddome has been limited. The goal of this bibliographic essay is to list the sources of this Cotswolds pastor to aid students of Beddome to gain familiarity with the relevant literature. By cataloguing his works, the hope is to show the development of Beddome studies since his death over two centuries ago.

This article will begin with writings from Beddome's own pen and other primary sources. Then, a historiography of Beddome will be given—these will be various biographical studies during the nineteenth, and bulk of the twentieth, centuries. In the final section, it will be demonstrated that there has been a resurgence of Beddome studies over the past three decades. These recent works on Beddome will be considered thematically—works on Beddome's biography, hymnody, and theology.

Primary sources

During his lifetime, the eighteenth-century Baptist pastor published very few

---

Devotion: Now First Published, from the Manuscripts of the Late Rev. B. Beddome, A.M. (London: Burton and Briggs; Button and Son, 1818), v–vii.

4 John Rippon, in the first obituary on Beddome, wrote, "How acceptable his labours were to the churches, when he could be prevailed on to visit them, has long been known at Abingdon, Bristol, London, and in the circle of the Midland Association" (John Rippon, "Rev. Benjamin Beddome, A. M. Bourton-on-the-Water, Gloucestershire," *Baptist Annual Register* 2 [1794–1797]: 322).

5 For the details concerning the widespread usage of Beddome's catechism, see below.

6 Hall wrote of Beddome's remaining in Bourton, "Though he spent the principal part of a long life in a village retirement, he was eminent for his colloquial powers, in which he displayed the urbanity of the gentleman, and the erudition of the scholar, combined with a more copious vein of attic salt than any person it has been my lot to know" (Hall, "Recommendatory Preface," vi).

7 Michael A.G. Haykin, "Benjamin Beddome (1717–1795): His Life and His Hymns," in *Pulpit and People: Studies in Eighteenth-Century Baptist Life and Thought*, ed. John H. Y. Briggs (Eugene, OR: Wipf & Stock, 2009), 111.

works—they were mainly his catechism and two circular letters that he wrote for the Midland Association.[8] Beddome permitted several of his hymns to be printed before his death in 1795.[9] Most of his works, however, were published posthumously. We will consider Beddome's works in the order of their publication: his catechism, his letters, his sermons, and his hymns. This will be followed by other primary sources, including items held at the Angus Library and Archive, Regent's Park College, Oxford.

Following the practice of his forebearers, Beddome employed *The Baptist Catechism*—commonly attributed to Benjamin Keach (1640–1704)—in the earlier parts of his ministry. Apparently sensing some lack, however, he produced *A Scriptural Exposition of the Baptist Catechism by Way of Question and Answer*.[10] Beddome's version expands on the original by adding sub-questions and answers to each section. The widespread usage of Beddome's catechism can be seen in its adoption by the Bristol Academy—the principal training center for British Baptists in the eighteenth century—and several printings into the nineteenth century.[11] This is also corroborated by a circular letter of the Western Association in which *A Scriptural Catechism* is commended, and an appeal made for the churches to purchase copies to cover printing costs.[12]

---

8 Daniel S. Ramsey notes that there were only two works produced by Beddome during his life time, referring to the catechism and the 1765 circular letter of the Midland Association (Daniel S. Ramsey, "'The Blessed Spirit': An Analysis of the Pneumatology of Benjamin Beddome as an Early Evangelical" [PhD diss., The Southern Baptist Theological Seminary, 2017], 4). This is corroborated by Thomas Brooks—the pastor of the Baptist church at Bourton-on-the-Water in the mid-nineteenth century—who wrote, "Although Mr. Beddome was an indefatigable writer he published but little—his catechism, in 1752, which he employed at Bourton among adults as well as children … and the circular letter of 1765, were the only things he thus gave the world" (Thomas Brooks, *Pictures of the Past: The History of the Baptist Church, Bourton-on-the-Water* [London: Judd & Glass, 1861], 60). Stokes, however, records that Beddome also wrote the 1759 circular letter for the Midland Association and that this was "the first *printed* circular letter" (Williams Stokes, *The History of the Midland Association of Baptist Churches* [London: R. Theobald, 1855], 89).

9 Haykin provides the details of this: "He did allow thirteen of his hymns to be published in a hymnal edited by fellow Baptists John Ash (1724–1779) and Caleb Evans (1737–1791) in 1769, *A Collection of Hymns Adapted to Public Worship*. Twenty or so years later, thirty-six of them appeared in the first edition of John Rippon's *A Selection of Hymns from the Best Authors* (1787)" (Michael A.G. Haykin, "Benjamin Beddome [1717–1795] of Bourton-on-the-Water," in Benjamin Beddome, *A Scriptural Exposition of the Baptist Catechism* [1776; repr., Birmingham, AL: Solid Ground Christian Books, 2006], viii). This volume is a modern reprint of Beddome's catechism, with the biographical sketch by Haykin, and a new introduction by James Renihan.

10 Benjamin Beddome, *A Scriptural Exposition of the Baptist Catechism by Way of Question and Answer*, 2nd ed. (Bristol: W. Pine, 1776). During Beddome's lifetime, there were two editions of the catechism. The first was published in 1752, and the second—which is cited here—was published in 1776 and used by the Bristol Academy. During the nineteenth century, the catechism as printed once in the British Isles and twice in the United States. For details of these publications, see Michael A.G. Haykin, "Benjamin Beddome (1717–1795)," in *The British Particular Baptists, 1638–1910*, ed. Michael A.G. Haykin and Terry Wolever (Springfield, MO: Particular Baptist Press, 2018), 4:268, 273.

11 For the details of this paragraph, I am indebted to Haykin, "Benjamin Beddome (1717–1795)," 4:267–68.

12 The letter in question is the 1776 circular letter of the Western Association. I was not able to access the letter directly, but did find it transcribed in Gary Brady, "Exposition of the Catechism Commended in the West," *Benjamin Beddome 1717–1795* (blog), accessed January 29, 2024, https://benbeddome.blogspot.com/2020/11/exposition-of-catechism-commended-in.html.

While he had an impact through his catechism in other parts of England, Beddome belonged to the Midland Association, to which he made a significant contribution. He attended his first meeting in 1743 in Leominster—where he also preached his first association sermon—and his last appearance was in 1789 in Evesham.[13] According to Robert W. Oliver, Beddome preached the annual association sermon a total of seventeen times.[14] Beddome was also moderator on five occasions and was tasked with writing the circular letter on behalf of the association in 1753, 1759, and 1765.[15]

In addition to the circular letters are the personal letters of Beddome. A number of these are reproduced in Thomas Brooks' history of the Bourton Church, *Pictures of the Past*. The bulk of these are penned by Beddome's father, John: (1) on the occasion of his son's baptism (undated); (2) expressing hesitation about Benjamin being called to the ministry so hurriedly (May 21, 1740); (3) two letters urging the younger Beddome to preach softer and shorter (May 17, 1742, and August 6, 1742); (4) regarding Beddome's decision to go to Warwick or Bourton (July 1743 or after); (5) expressing regret to miss his son's ordination (the ordination took place on September 23, 1743); and (6) urging him to come and work in Bristol (October 28, 1748).[16] In addition, there are two more letters in *Pictures of the Past*: (1) to a sister Reynolds for being absent "so many months from the house and table of the Lord" (March 8, 1761) and (2) to the association lamenting the decline in membership over the past two decades (May 1786).[17]

There is also a significant correspondence between Beddome (and the Bourton church) and the Little Prescott Street Baptist Church, Goodman's Fields, in London. The London church had recently lost their pastor, Samuel Wilson (1702–1750), and so sought Beddome's services. In his memoir, the writer says that Beddome had

---

13 Stokes, *The History of the Midland Association*, 88–90.

14 Robert W. Oliver, *History of the English Calvinistic Baptists, 1771–1892: From John Gill to C.H. Spurgeon* (Carlisle, PA: Banner of Truth Trust, 2006), 26. Jason C. Montgomery, commenting on Oliver's remark, says, "This would have exceeded the allowable times a minister was permitted to preach. The standing policy of the Midland Association was to permit a minister to preach no more than one time every three years. A simple doing of the math from Beddome's first appearance as preacher in 1743 to his last in 1789, clearly shows the rule was stretched where Beddome was concerned" (Jason C. Montgomery, "Benjamin Beddome: The Fruitful Life and Evangelical Labor of a Forgotten Village Preacher" [PhD diss., The Southwestern Baptist Theological Seminary, 2018], 146–7). See also, Rippon, "Rev. Benjamin Beddome," 325.

15 These statistics are from Montgomery, "Benjamin Beddome," 147. Benjamin Beddome, *The Circular Letter from the Elders and Messengers of the Several Baptist Churches, Meeting at Aulcester, Etc.* (Pershore: R. Lewis [for the Midland Baptist Association], 1759); Idem, *The Circular Letter from the Elders and Messengers of the Several Baptist Churches, Meeting at Aulcester, Etc.* (Worcester: R. Lewis [for the Midland Baptist Association], 1765). The 1753 letter is transcribed into the Bourton church books (Montgomery, "Benjamin Beddome," 143n69). In the statistics table given by Stokes, Beddome is listed as the moderator in 1746, 1749, 1753, and 1771, and as the writer of the circular letter in 1759 (Stokes, *The History of the Midland Association*, 87–93).

16 Brooks, *Pictures of the Past*, 23–26. These letters also appear in Anonymous, "Memoir," in *Sermons Printed from the Manuscripts of the Late Rev. Benjamin Beddome, A. M. of Bourton-on-the-Water* (London: William Ball, 1835), viii–xix.

17 Brooks, *Pictures of the Past*, 54–55, 63–64.

formerly been in communion with them [the Goodman's Fields church], and was still much beloved and admired. In addition to prospects of honour, comfort, and emolument, much more flattering than were connected with his situation at Bourton, our author had to resist the most pressing solicitations, couched in every form of argument and entreaty. Upon them all he put a direct negative; but so solicitous were they, that, as a last resource, he committed the whole affair to the decision of the church at Bourton.[18]

There were seven letters that were exchanged between Bourton and London; the deacons of the Bourton church also crafted some of the letters.[19] In his history of the Bourton church, Brooks remarks, "Comparatively few ministers are ever called to pass through an ordeal as trying as the one disclosed in the above correspondence, and it may be safely affirmed, that none ever came out with more credit to themselves. By this circumstance, Mr. Beddome's uprightness, disinterestedness, and simplicity, are placed above suspicion."[20]

There are also extracts from six letters written by Beddome to unknown relatives during 1759–60; these were initially published in the *Evangelical Magazine* and more recently published in the *Journal for Andrew Fuller Studies*.[21]

Beddome was both a powerful preacher and a prolific hymn-writer and left behind a large collection of sermons and hymns, which were published posthumously. That Beddome was an able preacher is universally acknowledged. His first biographer, John Rippon (1751–1825), says of him, "The labours of this good man among his charge were unremitted and evangelical. He fed them with the finest of the wheat. No man in all his connections wrote more sermons, nor composed them with greater care—and this was true of him to the last weeks of his life."[22]

There is an account of a time when Beddome was to preach at a minister's meeting. The service had already begun, but Beddome had forgotten both his text and sermon, and his habit was to preach without notes. Rippon continues the account:

> And in the way from the pew to the pulpit, he leaned his head over the shoulder of the Rev. Mr. Davis, pastor of the place, and said, "Brother Davis, what must I preach from?" Mr. Davis, thinking he could not be at a loss, answered,

18 Anonymous, "Memoir," xx.

19 These letters can be found in Thomas Brooks, "Ministerial Changes a Hundred Years Ago," *Baptist Magazine* 51 (July 1859): 425–29; idem, "Ministerial Changes a Hundred Years Ago," *Baptist Magazine* 51 (August 1859): 482–87; and idem, *Pictures of the Past*, 32–47.

20 Brooks, *Pictures of the Past*, 47.

21 *The Evangelical Magazine* 8 (1800): 156, 197, 229–30, 272–3, 319, 370; Gray Brady, ed., "Extracts from Six Letters Written by Benjamin Beddome in 1759 and 1760," *Journal of Andrew Fuller Studies* 1 (September 2020): 59–65. There is also a letter *to* Beddome, written by Daniel Turner, see Gray Brady, ed., "Consolation in Spiritual Darkness: A Letter from Daniel Turner to Benjamin Beddome 1762," *Journal of Andrew Fuller Studies* 2 (February 2021): 59–70.

22 Rippon, "Rev. Benjamin Beddome," 320.

"Ask no foolish questions." This afforded him considerable relief. He turned immediately to Titus 3:9, "Avoid foolish questions"—and preached a remarkably methodical, correct, and useful discourse on it.[23]

This sermon was published as "Sketch of a Sermon by the Late Rev. B. Beddome, A. M. of Bourton," in *The Baptist Annual Register*.[24]

Clearly, Beddome was an able preacher and thus his posterity sought to preserve something of his pulpit ministry. There was a collection of eight tomes, as well as a ninth stand-alone volume, that were all published within four decades of his death. In the introduction to the stand-alone volume we get an insight into what is contained in those works. The writer of the memoir remarks how the sermons are mere sketches taken from Beddome's manuscripts and thus are not what he would have preached verbatim in the pulpit. The memorialist says, rather, that "they are the mere skeletons and hints, which he filled out in the pulpit, and preserved without the least design of publication."[25]

Two hundred and twenty-five of Beddome's sermons are extant. Sixty-seven are in *Sermons Printed from the Manuscripts of the Late Rev. Benjamin Beddome, A.M. of Bourton-on-the-Water*.[26] To this volume was affixed an anonymously written "memoir."[27] The remaining sermons were published in a collection of eight volumes—the first seven are titled, *Twenty Short Discourses, Adapted to Village Worship or the Devotions of the Family*, and the eighth, *Short Discourses, Adapted to Village Worship or the Devotions of the Family*.[28] As their titles indicate, these sermons

---

23 Rippon, "Rev. Benjamin Beddome," 321; a few emendations have been made to ease reading.

24 John Rippon, "Sketch of a Sermon by the Late Rev. B. Beddome, A.M. of Bourton," *Baptist Annual Register* 3 (1798–1801): 415–21.

25 Anonymous, "Memoir," xxvi.

26 Beddome, *Sermons Printed from the Manuscripts of the Late Rev. Benjamin Beddome*. A modern reprint of this work is Benjamin Beddome, *The Sermons of Benjamin Beddome*, vol. 1 (Knightstown, IN: Particular Baptist Heritage Books, 2022).

27 Anonymous, "Memoir," ix–xxviii.

28 Benjamin Beddome, *Twenty Short Discourses, Adapted to Village Worship or the Devotions of the Family*, 2nd ed., vol. 1 (Dunstable: J. W. Morris, 1807); idem, *Twenty Short Discourses, Adapted to Village Worship or the Devotions of the Family*, vol. 2 (Dunstable: J.W. Morris, 1807); idem, *Twenty Short Discourses, Adapted to Village Worship or the Devotions of the Family*, 6th ed., vol. 3 (London: Samuel Burton; Simpkin & Marshall, 1824); idem, *Twenty Short Discourses, Adapted to Village Worship or the Devotions of the Family*, 4th ed., vol. 4 (London: R. Clay; Burton and Smith, 1822); idem, *Twenty Short Discourses, Adapted to Village Worship or the Devotions of the Family*, vol. 5 (London: W. Simpkin and R. Marshall, 1833); idem, *Twenty Short Discourses, Adapted to Village Worship or the Devotions of the Family*, 5th ed., vol. 6 (London: W. Simpkin and R. Marshall, 1834); idem, *Twenty Short Discourses, Adapted to Village Worship or the Devotions of the Family*, vol. 7 (London: Samuel Burton, 1825); idem, *Short Discourses, Adapted to Village Worship or the Devotions of the Family*, vol. 8 (London: Samuel Burton, 1825). There were several publications of these volumes. Brady says, "between 1807 and 1820 a goodly number of his sermons were printed in a series of eight volumes ... The sermons went through several editions and in 1835 were reissued in a larger combined format with a fresh volume of 67 more sermons" (Brady, ed., "Extracts from Six Letters Written by Benjamin Beddome," 59). For information concerning the editions, also see Haykin, "Benjamin Beddome (1717–1795)," 4:273; Montgomery, "Benjamin Beddome," 26n62.

were intended for village worship and use in the home.[29]

It was the habit of the Bourton pastor to prepare a hymn that would be suitable to the subject of his sermons that would be sung at the close of the service.[30] Thus, preaching and hymnody were inseparable for Beddome. A brief account from Beddome's later years speak of his devotion to both: "It was his earnest desire not to be long laid aside from his beloved employment, and in this he was gratified; for having, during his infirmities, been carried to and from the chapel, where he preached sitting, he was confined only one Lord's day, and was composing a hymn for public worship only an hour before his death."[31] Eight hundred and thirty[32] of these hymns were published in 1818 by Robert Hall, Jr., *Hymns Adapted to Public Worship, or Family Devotion: Now First Published, from the Manuscripts of the Late Rev. B. Beddome, A.M.*[33] Hall also affixed two prefaces to the volume.[34]

Before moving to the secondary works of the nineteenth and the twentieth centuries, this section will conclude with a brief mention of other primary sources concerning Beddome. Rippon wrote the first biography on Beddome shortly after the Bourton pastor's death, which was an obituary for *The Baptist Annual Register*.[35]

Those desiring to do Beddome research should be aware of the material housed at the Angus Library and Archive, Regent's Park College, Oxford. A significant source of material, for example, are the *Bourton-on-the-Water Church Books*.[36]

---

29 Concerning village worship, a reviewer (not of Beddome's sermons) wrote, "Among other means of circulating divine truth, that of village preaching has long been considered as of great importance; and several preachers have perpetuated their instruction by the press, that those good and zealous men who have not the talent of preaching, may be furnished with discourses to read to their poor neighbours and acquaintance. ... Mr. Beddome and many other writers, have emulated [Mr. Burder] in the same walk of usefulness; and we hail every attempt of the kind" ("Review of Religious Publications, Sermons, chiefly designed for the Use of Villages and Families. By Thornhill Kidd," *Evangelical Magazine and Missionary Chronicle* 22 [June 1814]: 217).

30 Hall, "Recommendatory Preface," ix.

31 Anonymous, "Memoir," xxv.

32 Haykin says that these were "822 hymns and 8 doxologies" (Haykin, "Benjamin Beddome [1717–1795] of Bourton-on-the-Water," viii).

33 Beddome, *Hymns Adapted to Public Worship, or Family Devotion*. A modern reprint of this work is Benjamin Beddome, *Hymns Adapted to Public Worship or Family Devotion: A New Edition Including Hymns Not in 1818 Book and Hymns Published Earlier*, ed. Robert Hall, Jr. and Barry C. Johnston (1818; repr., London: Burton and Briggs; Button and Son, 2020).

34 Hall, "Recommendatory Preface," v–viii; Hall, "Editor's Preface," in *Hymns Adapted to Public Worship, or Family Devotion*, ix.

35 Rippon, "Rev. Benjamin Beddome," 314–26. The *Register* is an important work for studying Beddome as it provides background information concerning the English Particular Baptist denomination during a critical period of their history. Ken Manley says, "The thirteen years during which Rippon published his *Register* were among the most significant in the history of the Particular Baptists in both Britain and the United States" (Ken Manley, *Redeeming Love Proclaim: John Rippon and the Baptists* [Carlisle, UK: Paternoster, 2004], 139).

36 There are three volumes: *Bourton-on-the-Water Church Book 1719–1802* (Angus Library and Archive, Regent's Park College, Oxford); *Bourton-on-the-Water Church Book 1745–1773* (Angus Library and Archive, Regent's Park College, Oxford); *Bourton-on-the-Water Church Book 1765–1920* (Angus Library and Archive, Regent's Park College, Oxford).

These capture church minutes, conversion accounts, instances of church discipline, changes in membership, letters written to the association, a transcription of the circular letters, and business of the church (e.g., the church calling Beddome as their "preaching elder").[37]

In addition to the church books, the Angus Library holds volumes of Beddome's sermons; the Bourton pastor's personal library of six hundred plus volumes; several letters;[38] manuscripts of his hymns; notes to a sermon; and minutes of the Midland Association.[39] Of course, a trip to Oxford may be an obstacle for many. However, serious students of Beddome, and particularly doctoral candidates, would be immensely helped by a visit to the Angus Library.[40]

Historiography of Beddome

In this section, the various biographical studies from the nineteenth and a good part of the twentieth centuries will be listed. The literature on Beddome is not legion. He did not receive extensive treatment by church historians, Baptist or otherwise.[41] There were, though, a handful of works that emerged in the nineteenth century. Some were introductory works affixed to his hymns and sermons; these were mentioned with the respective primary sources above. J.L. Reynolds also wrote an introduction for the 1849 edition of *A Scriptural Catechism*.[42] However, this was nearly a century after Beddome's initial publication of his catechism, and so is included here. Reynolds' introduction provides a sketch of Beddome's life and a brief apology for catechetical instruction.

Joseph Ivimey (1773–1834) included a biography of Beddome in *A History of the English Baptists Comprising the Principal Events of the History of the Protestant Dissenters, during the Reign of Geo. III* in 1830.[43] A few decades later, Thomas

---

37 Since I do not have access to the church books, I am indebted to others for my understanding of what is recorded in them; e.g., Haykin, "Benjamin Beddome (1717–1795)," 4:263, 265–7; Montgomery, "Benjamin Beddome," 127–9, 136–9, 143–6.

38 Benjamin Beddome, Letter to Anne Steele, December 23, 1742; Beddome, Letter to Richard Hall, February 18, 1764; Beddome, Letter to Andrew Fuller, October [2?], 1793; and Beddome, Letter to John Collett Ryland, n.d. The titles of these letters can be found through a search on the Angus Library archive search.

39 For the details listed here, I am relying on Gary Brady, "Sources–What's Where," *Benjamin Beddome 1717–1795* (blog), assessed June 29, 2010, https://benbeddome.blogspot.com/2010/06/what-is-where.html). In the same post, he notes a few other items available at the Bristol Baptist College Library, the Dr. Williams' Library in London, the Gloucestershire Record Office, and the National Library of Wales. Admittedly, a gap in this article is that it does not consider the unique sources that can be found in these other libraries and archives.

40 A visit to Bourton-on-the-Water would be practical also since it is less than an hour's drive from Oxford.

41 This statement should be tempered, at least concerning the nineteenth century, by the fact that much of Beddome's own works were published during the 1800s.

42 J.L. Reynolds, "Introduction," in Benjamin Beddome, *A Scriptural Exposition of the Baptist Catechism, by Way of Question and Answers* (Richmond: Harold & Murray, 1849), 3–27.

43 Joseph Ivimey, *A History of the English Baptists: Comprising the Principal Events of the History of the Protestant Dissenters, during the Reign of Geo. III* (London: Isaac Taylor Hinton and Holdsworth & Ball, 1830), 4:461–69. The work by Ivimey, though, is largely a reproduction of Rippon's work according to Haykin (Haykin, "Benjamin Beddome [1717–1795],"

Brooks—pastor of the Bourton church during the nineteenth century—published *Pictures of the Past: The History of the Baptist Church, Bourton-on-the-Water*. This history covers the period from the church's inception through to the author's own day (1655–1861), and Beddome is the focus of four chapters.[44] Stephen Albert Swaine wrote a short biography in *Faithful Men; or, Memorials of Bristol College, and Some of its Most Distinguished Alumni*.[45] Montgomery says the work presents Beddome as "associated with a virtual 'Who's Who' listing of evangelical Calvinistic ministers."[46] Short biographical sketches were also written by Hester in *The Baptist Magazine*, Joseph Belcher in *Historical Sketches of Hymns, Their Writers, and Their Influence*, and J.M. Cramp in *Baptist History from the Foundation of the Christian Church to the Close of the Eighteenth Century*.[47]

Turning to the twentieth century, the most important work was Derrick Holmes' "The Early Years (1655–1740) of Bourton-on-the-Water Dissenters Who Later Constituted the Baptist Church, with Special Reference to the Ministry of the Reverend Benjamin Beddome A.M. 1740–1795."[48] The dissertation begins with Beddome's early years, education, and call to the Baptist church at Bourton-on-the-Water. Interestingly, it includes a short chapter on the catchment area of the membership, which shows that the church drew people from a twenty-file mile radius of Bourton-on-the-Water.[49] There are also chapters on the church's practice of discipline, men called to the ministry under Beddome's pastorate, the correspondence between Beddome and the Goodman's Fields Church, his literary corpus, and Beddome's assistant Mr. Wilkins who was rather discontent in Bourton. Of this study, Daniel S. Ramsey indicates that Holmes "has donesome important historical research in and around Bourton-on-the-Water. His findings have proven beneficial in understanding the historical context in which Beddome's ministry took place and the physical environment that influenced daily life there. Holmes has also done research into the Bourton church records, which shed further light

---

4:272).

44 Brooks, *Pictures of the Past*, 21–66.

45 Stephen Albert Swaine, *Faithful Men; or, Memorials of Bristol Baptist College, and Some of Its Most Distinguished Alumni* (London: Alexander & Shepheard, 1884), 42–47.

46 Montgomery, "Benjamin Beddome," 5.

47 G. Hester, "Baptist Worthies—Benjamin Beddome," *Baptist Magazine* 57 (July 1865): 441–6; Joseph Belcher, *Historical Sketches of Hymns, Their Writers, and Their Influence* (Philadelphia: Lindsay & Blakiston, 1859), 83–85; J.M. Cramp, *Baptist History from the Foundation of the Christian Church to the Close of the Eighteenth Century* (Philadelphia: American Baptist Publication Society, 1869), 519–21.

48 Derrick Holmes, "The Early Years (1655–1740) of Bourton-on-the-Water Dissenters Who Later Constituted the Baptist Church, with Special Reference to the Ministry of the Reverend Benjamin Beddome A.M. 1740–1795" (Unpublished Certificate in Education Dissertation, St. Paul's College, 1969). Haykin says, "In this century there have been relatively few studies of Beddome. The most important is that of Derrick Holmes" (Michael A.G. Haykin, "'Glory to the Three Eternal': Benjamin Beddome and the Teaching of Trinitarian Theology in the Eighteenth Century," *Southern Baptist Journal of Theology* 10.1 [2006]: 82n24).

49 Holmes, "The Early Years (1655–1740) of Bourton-on-the-Water Dissenters," 32–34.

on Beddome's writings and conclusions."⁵⁰

Also in the twentieth century, Kenneth Dix wrote an article that focused on the exchange between Beddome and the Goodman's Fields church called "'Thy Will Be Done': A Study in the Life of Benjamin Beddome," for *The Bulletin of the Strict Baptist Historical Society*, and David R. Breed included Beddome in *The History and Use of Hymns and Hymn-Tunes*, listing him as the first author in "Hymns of the Second Period."⁵¹

Resurgence of Beddome studies

Over the past thirty years, there has been a resurgence in Beddome studies, with Baptist historian Michael A.G. Haykin being the main catalyst for that renewal. Though Haykin is best known for his role in the revival of interest in Beddome's later (and more significant) contemporary Andrew Fuller (1754–1815), because of his research interest in the British Particular Baptists of the long eighteenth century, Haykin has written regularly on the Bourton pastor.⁵² Due to this renewed interest in Beddome, more works have been written in the last thirty years than in the preceding two centuries. This section of the essay will be organized according to various aspects of Beddome and his thought. First, biographical pieces will be listed, with a brief word about the work of pastor-blogger, Gary Brady. Then, works on Beddome's hymnody and thought (or theology) will be catalogued. This section will conclude with the most important monograph on Beddome to date.

In 1998, Haykin wrote a helpful biographical sketch, "Benjamin Beddome (1717–1795)" in an anthology he edited, *The British Particular Baptists, 1638–1910*.⁵³ Haykin overviews the Cotswold pastor's life, relating his upbringing, conversion, ministerial training, call to Bourton, marriage, and the numerical increase and decline of the church. Interesting details are included, such as the cost of the manse, which was built by the church after Beddome's marriage to Elizabeth Boswell. Specific incidents are recorded as well—for example, the conversion of Ann Wakefield and the strange account of a sister Hardiman who came under church discipline for her improper behavior.⁵⁴ The chapter concludes with a bibliography of primary and secondary sources on Beddome.⁵⁵ Haykin also wrote a short bio-

---

50 Ramsey, "'The Blessed Spirit,'" 3–4.

51 Kenneth Dix, "'Thy Will Be Done': A Study in the Life of Benjamin Beddome," *Bulletin of the Strict Baptist Historical Society* 9 (1972): n.p.; David R. Breed, *The History and Use of Hymns and Hymn-Tunes* (Chicago: Fleming H. Revell Company, 1903), 149–53.

52 What Nathan A. Finn says of Haykin regarding Fuller studies—that he "emerged as the key scholar engaging a wide range of Fuller's theology and legacy"—could similarly be said of him concerning Beddome studies (Finn, "The Renaissance in Andrew Fuller Studies," 48).

53 Michael A.G. Haykin, ed. "Benjamin Beddome (1717–1795)," in *The British Particular Baptists, 1638–1910*, ed. Michael A.G. Haykin (Springfield, MO: Particular Baptist Press, 1998), 1:167–83; this was slightly adapted and republished as Haykin, "Benjamin Beddome (1717–1795)," 4:258–73.

54 Haykin, "Benjamin Beddome (1717–1795)," 4:264–7.

55 Haykin, "Benjamin Beddome (1717–1795)," 4:272–3.

graphical sketch, "Benjamin Beddome (1717–1795) of Bourton-on-the-Water," as an introduction to the reprint of *A Scriptural Exposition of the Baptist Catechism*.[56] A similar version of this was previously published in three parts by *Evangelical Times*: "A Cloud of Witnesses--Benjamin Beddome."[57]

Other biographical works appeared during this resurgence period. Robert W. Oliver devoted a chapter to Beddome in *History of the English Calvinistic Baptists, 1771–1892: from John Gill to C.H. Spurgeon*.[58] Luke David wrote a "Biographical Preface: The Life and Times of Benjamin Beddome (1717–1798)," to *The Sermons of Benjamin Beddome*, which is a reprint of the 1835 standalone volume of his sermons.[59] Most recently, Stephen Pickles wrote a full-length biography, *The Life and Times of Benjamin Beddome*.[60] The book follows mostly a chronological order, with certain important documents and themes weaved throughout. Pickles has done a service for those engaged in Beddome studies by pulling together a massive amount of material into this one volume.

In studying Beddome, the contribution of Gary Brady should not be overlooked. Brady is the pastor of Childs Hill Baptist Church in London and has taken a keen interest in Beddome who he says is a "lesser light."[61] Due to his extensive research and writing, Brady has become of the leading experts on the eighteenth-century Bourton pastor.[62] He hosts a website that contains hundreds of posts concerning the life, preaching, hymnody, correspondence, and pastoral ministry of Beddome.[63] Thus, the student of Beddome should consult Brady's blog as a starting point, even though the medium is not academic *per se*.[64] In terms of published biographical works, Brady makes two significant contributions. First, he contributed a

---

56 Haykin, "Benjamin Beddome (1717–1795) of Bourton-on-the-Water," i–x.

57 Michael A.G. Haykin, "A Cloud of Witnesses--Benjamin Beddome (Part 1)," *Evangelical Times* (July 1, 2001); Haykin, "A Cloud of Witnesses--Benjamin Beddome (Part 2)," *Evangelical Times* (August 1, 2001); Haykin, "A Cloud of Witnesses--Benjamin Beddome (3)," *Evangelical Times* (September 1, 2001).

58 Oliver, *History of the English Calvinistic Baptists*, 16–29.

59 Luke David, "Biographical Preface: The Life and Times of Benjamin Beddome (1717–1795)," in *Sermons of Benjamin Beddome*, 1:xi–xxix.

60 Stephen Pickles, *Cotswolds Pastor and Baptist Hymn Writer: The Life and Times of Benjamin Beddome* (Upham, UK: James Bourne Society, 2023).

61 Gary Brady, "Benjamin Beddome 1717–1795," in *My Kingdom Is Not of This World: Papers Read at the 2021 Westminster Conference* (London: Westminster Conference, 2022), 145.

62 Ramsey says of Brady that he is "one of the most prolific students of Beddome today" (Ramsey, "The Blessed Spirit," 4).

63 Ramsey, "The Blessed Spirit," 4. Gary Brady, "Benjamin Beddome 1717–1795," accessed January 25, 2024, http://benbeddome.blogspot.com/.

64 To cite just a few examples of the helpfulness of Brady's blog: he has a series of posts on the contents of Beddome's library which are housed at the Angus Library; he has a post on the full chronology of Beddome's life, which is periodically updated; he has reproduced many primary sources, e.g., Midland Association letters; and he has a post on extant letters to and from Beddome, listing where the researcher can access the letters.

chapter in the monograph *Glory to the Three Eternal*, "Being Benjamin Beddome."[65] Second, he presented a paper at the 2021 Westminster Conference which was published as "Benjamin Beddome 1717–1795" in *My Kingdom is not of this World*.[66] Brady tells his personal story of how he came to be invested in Beddome before providing a biographical sketch; this is followed by thematic reflections on the pastoral ministry of the Cotswolds pastor, and a bibliography.

The above works are biographical. They deal with the events of Beddome's life—chronicling his successes and trials—and recount his upbringing, ministerial training, his call and commitment to the church, his family, and his practices during his fifty-five-year pastorate in Bourton-on-the-Water. Over the past thirty years, as interest in Beddome grew, there were several specific studies that emerged. These will now be considered in two categories: an analysis of Beddome's hymnody and that of his thought, or theology.

First, several pieces were written on Beddome's hymnody. In the 1990s, Richard Arnold devoted a chapter to Beddome's hymns in *English Hymns of the Eighteenth Century: An Anthology*, and J.R. Watson included a brief section in *The English Hymn: A Critical and Historical Study*.[67] Anthony R. Cross gives a substantial treatment in *Useful Learning: Neglected Means of Grace in the Reception of the Evangelical Revival among English Particular Baptists*.[68] Haykin has contributed three pieces on Beddome's hymnody; these are two articles—"Baptists Reflecting on Adam & Eve in the 'Long' Eighteenth Century," and "'Drawn in Crimson Lines': Colour in the Hymnody of Benjamin Beddome"—and a chapter in *Pulpit and People: Studies in Eighteenth-Century Baptist Life and Thought*—"Benjamin Beddome (1717–1795): His Life and His Hymns."[69]

Turning now to works on Beddome's thought, or theology, there is Roger Hayden's dissertation, "Evangelical Calvinism among Eighteenth-century British Baptists with Particular Reference to Bernard Foskett, Hugh and Caleb Evans and the Bristol Baptist Academy, 1690–1791," which was later published as a monograph: *Continuity and Change: Evangelical Calvinism Among Eighteenth-century Baptist Ministers Trained at Bristol Academy, 1690–1791*.[70] Both are a study of the

---

65 Gary Brady, "Being Benjamin Beddome: A Biographical Study," in *Glory to the Three Eternal: Tercentennial Essays on the Life and Writings of Benjamin Beddome (1718–1795)*, ed. Michael A.G. Haykin, Roy M. Paul, and Jeongmo Yoo (Eugene, OR: Pickwick, 2019), 1–33.

66 Brady, "Benjamin Beddome," 1–33.

67 J.R. Watson, *The English Hymn: A Critical and Historical Study* (Oxford: Oxford University Press, 1997), 198–202; Richard Arnold, ed., *English Hymns of the Eighteenth Century: An Anthology* (New York: Peter Lang, 1991), 360–8.

68 Anthony R. Cross, *Useful Learning: Neglected Means of Grace in the Reception of the Evangelical Revival among English Particular Baptists* (Eugene, OR: Wipf and Stock, 2017), 57–70. Montgomery says of Cross' work that it is "the most comprehensive work to date on the hymnody of Beddome" (Montgomery, "Benjamin Beddome," 10).

69 Michael A.G. Haykin, "Baptists Reflecting on Adam & Eve in the 'Long' Eighteenth Century," *Southern Baptist Journal of Theology* 15.1 (2011): 92–99; idem, "'Drawn in Crimson Lines': Colour in the Hymnody of Benjamin Beddome," *Puritan Reformed Journal* 14.2 (July 2022): 60–64; idem, "Benjamin Beddome (1717–1795): His Life and His Hymns," 93–111.

70 Roger Hayden, "Evangelical Calvinism among Eighteenth-Century British Baptists with Particular Reference to

eighteenth-century English Particular Baptists, the denomination to which Beddome belonged. In Hayden's words:

> This thesis challenges the commonly received view of eighteenth-century Particular Baptists as obscurantist, ill-educated hyper-Calvinists. From the very beginning Particular Baptists had been evangelical in their Calvinism. In the seventeenth century this was true of all Particular Baptists who shared the *1644 Confession of Faith* and sought to promulgate it in various parts of the country. At the end of the century this evangelical Calvinism still gripped the minds and hearts of many Particular Baptists in the Western Association, based upon Bristol; and under the leadership of Bernard Foskett in the next century evangelical Calvinism was vigorously continued by those who came into contact with him and the students he trained at the Bristol Academy.[71]

Hayden examines the theology of the denomination through its various associations, ministerial training school, and theology and activity of missions. The main figures considered are three principals of the Bristol Academy—Bernard Foskett (1685–1758), Hugh Evans (1712–1781), and Caleb Evans (1737–1791).[72] However, Beddome also receives significant treatment with an examination of his life, catechism, and hymns.[73] This is not surprising since Beddome's father, John, and Foskett were friends, and the younger Beddome was trained at the Bristol Academy.

In the twenty-first century, there were two doctoral dissertations on Beddome, both focusing on an aspect of his theology. In the introduction to his dissertation, Jason M. Montgomery said, "What Hayden's work has done for Foskett and the Evans's, this work hopes to do for Beddome."[74] Thus, Montgomery argues for the evangelical theology of Beddome—namely, that he believed that the gospel was to be freely offered to all people and was convinced that all people have a duty to be believe in contrast to the hyper Calvinism of his day. Thus, there is a continuity between the stream of evangelical Calvinism—present in the seventeenth-century

---

Bernard Foskett, Hugh and Caleb Evans and the Bristol Baptist Academy, 1690–1791" (PhD diss., University of Keele, 1991); *idem, Continuity and Change: Evangelical Calvinism Among Eighteenth-Century Baptist Ministers Trained at Bristol Academy, 1690–1791* (Chipping Norton, UK: Nigel Lynn, 2006). For a short article on Foskett's impact, see Roger Hayden, "The Contribution of Bernard Foskett," in *Pilgrim Pathways: Essays in Baptist History in Honour of B.R. White*, ed. William H. Brackney, Paul S. Fiddes, and John H.Y. Briggs (Macon, GA: Mercer University Press, 1999), 189–206.

71 Hayden, *Continuity and Change*, xi.

72 Haykin says, "The Bristol Baptist Academy [was] the sole British Baptist seminary for much of the eighteenth century" (Haykin, "Glory to the Three Eternal," 77). For the history and impact of the Bristol Academy, see John Rippon, *A Brief Essay towards an History of the Baptist Academy at Bristol* (London: Dilly and Button; Brown, James, and Cottell, 1796); Jeongmo Yoo, "The Bristol Academy and the Education of Ministers in Eighteenth-Century England (1758–1791)," in *Church and School in Early Modern Protestantism: Studies in Honor of Richard A. Muller on the Maturation of a Theological Tradition*, ed. Jordan J. Ballor, David S. Sytsma, and Jason Zuidema (Leiden: Brill, 2013); David W. Bebbington, "The Significance of Bristol Baptist College," *Baptist Quarterly* 53.4 (2022): 149–66.

73 Hayden, *Continuity and Change*, 80–91, 154–8, 168–72.

74 Montgomery, "Benjamin Beddome," 13.

Particular Baptists and the Bristol Tradition under Foskett and the Evans's—and Beddome.[75] Montgomery's dissertation was titled, "Benjamin Beddome: The Fruitful Life and Evangelical Labor of a Forgotten Village Preacher."[76] Daniel S. Ramsey wrote, "'The Blessed Spirit': An Analysis of the Pneumatology of Benjamin Beddome as an Early Evangelical."[77] In his dissertation, Ramsey demonstrates the continuity of Beddome's pneumatology with that of his Reformed, Puritan, and Baptist forebearers.

In addition to the above dissertations, there was a master's thesis by Stephen Mckay, "The Trinitarian Theology of Particular Baptists in England (1734–1795): Anne Dutton, Benjamin Beddome, Caleb Evans, and Samuel Stennett."[78] Addressing a similar topic, Huafang Xu wrote a dissertation on the Trinitarian spirituality of Anne Dutton (1692–1765)—"Communion with God and Comfortable Dependence on Him: Anne Dutton's Trinitarian Spirituality"—where Beddome's catechism and hymns are analyzed in a chapter on the Trinitarian theology of eighteenth-century English Particular Baptists.[79]

Haykin also wrote on Beddome's theology, specifically his views on the Trinity, the Bible, and earthly rulers: "'Glory to the Three Eternal': Benjamin Beddome and the Teaching of Trinitarian Theology in the Eighteenth Century," "Benjamin Beddome and the Bible," and "'Nursing Fathers and … Nursing Mothers to the Israel of God': Benjamin Beddome on Praying for Godly Rulers."[80] Haykin has also written: "'Those Who Plead for Thee': English Particular Baptist Preaching in the Long Eighteenth Century," which examines the preaching of Beddome and his contemporaries like Hall and Fuller.[81]

Peter Naylor included a brief section on Beddome's views on communion in *Calvinism, Communion, and the Baptists: A Study of English Calvinistic Baptists from the Late 1600s to the Early 1800s*, and Brady wrote two articles on "Benjamin Beddome and Friendship" in the *Banner of Truth Magazine*.[82]

---

75 Montgomery, "Benjamin Beddome," 7–8.

76 Montgomery, "Benjamin Beddome."

77 Ramsey, "'The Blessed Spirit.'"

78 Stephen Mckay, "The Trinitarian Theology of Particular Baptists in England (1734–1795): Anne Dutton, Benjamin Beddome, Caleb Evans, and Samuel Stennett" (Master's thesis, Australian College of Theology, 2019).

79 Huafang Xu, "Communion with God and Comfortable Dependence on Him: Anne Dutton's Trinitarian Spirituality" (PhD diss., The Southern Baptist Theological Seminary, 2018), 44–66.

80 Haykin, "Glory to the Three Eternal"; Michael A. G. Haykin, "Benjamin Beddome and the Bible," *Evangelical Times* 51.2 (2017): 12–15; Haykin, "'Nursing Fathers and … Nursing Mothers to the Israel of God': Benjamin Beddome on Praying for Godly Rulers," *Journal of Andrew Fuller Studies* 7 (September 2023): 65–68.

81 Michael A.G. Haykin, "'Those Who Plead for Thee': English Particular Baptist Preaching in the Long Eighteenth Century," *Evangelical Quarterly* 94.4 (2023): 299–311.

82 Peter Naylor, *Calvinism, Communion, and the Baptists: A Study of English Calvinistic Baptists from the Late 1600s to the Early 1800s* (Carlisle, UK: Paternoster, 2003), 53–54; Gary Brady, "Benjamin Beddome on Friendship (Part 1)," *Banner of Truth Magazine* (October 2023); Brady, "Benjamin Beddome on Friendship (Part 2)," *Banner of Truth Magazine* (November 2023).

Certainly, the most significant work on Beddome to date is the monograph edited by Haykin, Roy M. Paul, and Jeongmo Yoo, *Glory to the Three Eternal: Tercentennial Essays on the Life and Writings of Benjamin Beddome (1718–1795)*.[83] In the monograph, which was published in 2019, Gary Brady gives a biographical sketch; Haykin adapted his article on Beddome's Trinitarian theology; Yoo wrote a chapter on the Bourton pastor's Christology; Ramsey and Montgomery provide shorter versions of their dissertations—on Beddome's pneumatology and his evangelicalism, respectively; and R. Scott Connell considers his hymnody.[84] The publication of this volume, according to Haykin, was "the realization of a personal dream, which gripped [him] sometime in the early 1990s."[85] Written for the tercentennial anniversary of his birth, this collection brings together the fruit of the most important recent work on Beddome into a single volume.

Conclusion

This bibliographic essay has sought to capture the major primary and secondary sources on Benjamin Beddome. The Bourton pastor died in 1795 and given that most of his works were published posthumously, several publications of his works did emerge in the nineteenth century. Thus, Beddome's catechism, hymns, and sermons were known and used for many decades after his passing. For example, the last printing of his catechism was in 1849 (in the United States) and nearly a hundred of his hymns appeared in hymnals at the end of the nineteenth century.[86] In the twentieth century, though, Beddome was forgotten, and so few works were published.

Beginning in the 1990s, there was a renewed interest in Beddome. Roger Hayden's 1991 dissertation—"Evangelical Calvinism among Eighteenth-century British Baptists"—serves as a helpful marker for this renewal. This dissertation, however, is not focused primarily on Beddome, and the catalyst for this resurgence in Beddome studies has been Michael A.G. Haykin. He wrote a helpful biographical sketch in 1998 and has continued to write regularly on the Bourton pastor. This has culminated in the publication of *Glory to the Three Eternal*, the only monograph on Beddome to date.

This bibliographic essay purposefully aims to raise awareness of the forgotten Beddome. For his own generation, Beddome was an effective and fruitful pastor, and his writings continued to bless many even decades after his death. He was an able preacher, skilled hymn-writer, and an effective catechizer, which is reflected in the preservation of his sermons, hymns, and catechism by later generations. Beyond his own church, he was an active and well-respected pastor in the Midland Association, and several men were called to the ministry who were associated with

---

83 Haykin, Paul, and Yoo, eds., *Glory to the Three Eternal*.

84 Haykin, "Preface," in *Glory to the Three Eternal*, xii.

85 Haykin, "Preface," xii.

86 Haykin, "Benjamin Beddome (1717–1795)," 4:268, 271.

the Bourton church.[87]

Yet, Beddome was what Brady calls a "lesser light." As Brady argues, "When selecting a figure from church history [to study], the obvious thing is to choose a great—Owen, Edwards, Andrew Fuller. However, there is merit in studying lesser lights. It at least means studying someone you can hope to emulate, rather than a giant you will only ever admire from afar."[88] Beddome's similarity to the ordinary pastor can be illustrated in three ways. First, while his church saw growth during his fifty-five-year pastorate, it also saw periods of decline. In the final three decades of his ministry—from 1764 to 1795—the membership at the Bourton church had a net loss of sixty members.[89] Second, there is the unique collection of letters between Beddome and the Goodman's Fields church in London. The latter desired Beddome to be their pastor, but Beddome refused the invitation. He felt called to the Bourton church and was compelled to stay even if that meant being in a less useful or lower station.[90] There are lessons to be learned from that correspondence. Third, while Beddome did experience revival earlier in his ministry, he ministered, according to Haykin, "between the times—those times of Baptist advance in the seventeenth century and those of revival in the final couple of decades of the eighteenth century."[91] This resembles the context of many Christians in this generation who enjoy little obvious fruit, yet are seeking to be faithful to Christ in the ordinary course of life and ministry. More works on Beddome are in need and may the renaissance continue.

---

87 Rippon, "Rev. Benjamin Beddome," 323.

88 Brady, "Benjamin Beddome 1717–1795," 145.

89 This was from 183 to 123 members. Brooks, *Pictures of the Past*, 50, 55. Haykin, "Benjamin Beddome (1717–1795)," 4:264–65.

90 Beddome wrote in his last letter to the Goodman's Fields church, "If the prospect of greater usefulness is in itself a sufficient plea for the removal which you press, then it would be impossible for churches of a lower rank ever to be secure of the continuance of their pastors … I am determined that I will not violently rend myself from them, for I would rather honour God in a much lower station than that in which he hath placed me, than intrude myself into a higher without his direction" (Brooks, *Pictures of the Past*, 46–47).

91 Haykin, "Benjamin Beddome (1717–1795)," 4:263; *idem*, "Benjamin Beddome (1717–1795): His Life and His Hymns," 111.

The Journal of Andrew Fuller Studies
8 | Spring 2024

John Fawcett on anger

Anna Carini

Anna Carini is currently pursuing doctoral studies in biblical spirituality at The Southern Baptist Theological Seminary. Her area of research is the life and theology of John Fawcett.

John Fawcett was an English Calvinistic Baptist minister who lived from 1739–1817 and is primarily known today for his hymn writing. He grew up in the Church of England and was greatly impacted by the preaching of George Whitefield, then became a Baptist minister. Fawcett's story is one of great humility and loyalty to one congregation throughout a minister's career. He became an ordained Baptist pastor at Wainsgate in 1765 at the age of 26, and his successful ministry and preaching became known around England, and he was close friends with other well-known ministers such as Andrew Fuller. In 1772, he was invited to replace the famous pastor John Gill who had just died the previous year at Carter's Lane Baptist Church in London. The pay increase would have been great if he accepted the call, and after his wagons were loaded with his family's possessions, the tears of his congregants made him change his mind and decide to stay at his poor, country Baptist church. In 1793, he was once again invited to a more prestigious calling to become President of the Baptist Academy at Bristol but declined and remained at his Wainsgate church and then at Hebdenbridge in the parish of Halifax till his death in 1817, serving there for 54 years. Fawcett's most famous hymn, "Blest Be the Tie That Binds," expresses his love for church, though the timing of when he wrote it is not certain. The first stanza says, "Blest be the tie that binds/our hearts in Christian love;/the fellowship of kindred minds/is like to that above," and continues to focus on the love among Christians in a church.

Little has been written about Fawcett, but most has focused on his contribution to hymn-writing. However, Fawcett also wrote *An Essay on Anger*, which impressed George III (1738–1820) and is an example of Fawcett's rich theology of the passions.[1]

---

1 Michael A.G. Haykin, *"Blest Be the Tie that Binds": Remembering John Fawcett, His Times, His Life, His Hymn* (Louis-

This paper examines the riches of Fawcett's work on anger in how he draws from the historical tradition of the passions and works of ancient philosophy, and how he applies these ideas to the areas of the home and Christian unity.

A biographical sketch of Fawcett

The main primary sources of information on Fawcett are from an account of his life written by his son, John Fawcett, Jr., published in 1818 and an anonymous memoir of the author written as a forward to Fawcett's *Miscellaneous Works* published in 1824. Fawcett was born in Yorkshire to Stephen Fawcett who died when his son was only 12, leaving his wife as a single mother to many. The pain and fear of his father's death though led him to seek what the truth of what mankind's final state may be. Fawcett, Jr. wrote that "These painful apprehensions led him fervently to supplicate the Divine throne for relief and consolation."[2] His anxiety about death led him to read many Puritan books such as Bunyan's *Pilgrim's Progress*, Richard Baxter's *Call to the Unconverted* and the anonymously written *The Whole Duty of Man*. At the age of thirteen, he became an apprentice at Bradford for the next six years where he worked from six in the morning till eight at night but still found time to read and be ministered to by a Butler at the Bradford church.[3] He was also mentored by David Pratt who taught him Latin and gave him an informal education through many valuable books and discussions.[4]

When Pratt died suddenly, Fawcett was then attracted to the ministry for George Whitfield, John and Charles Wesley, and William Grimshaw who were all active and influential ministers in England.[5] At around sixteen, Fawcett first heard Whitefield preach from John 3:14 about Moses lifting up the serpent in the wilderness to a large crowd in the open air in Bradford and wrote of the experience, "As long as life remains, I shall remember both the text and the sermon."[6] Hearing this sermon was a kind of conversion experience for Fawcett, even though he had been hearing sermons and reading spiritual works. Fawcett wrote of the experience, "In the sixteenth year of my age, it pleased God graciously, and more particularly than ever before, to work upon my mind, and to give me a deeper sense of my lost condition by nature. I think it was about the month of September 1755."[7] He began associating more with the Methodists and attending their meetings and always returning to hear Whitefield preach when he came north. The Anglican ministers

---

ville, KY: Andrew Fuller Center for Baptist Studies, 2018), 10.

2 John Fawcett, Jr., *An Account of the Life, Ministry, and Writings of the Late Rev. John Fawcett, D.D.* (London: Baldwin, Cradock, and Joy; Halifax: P.K. Holden, 1818), 7.

3 Fawcett, Jr., *Life, Ministry, and Writings*, 12.

4 Fawcett, Jr., *Life, Ministry, and Writings*, 12.

5 Fawcett, Jr., *Life, Ministry, and Writings*, 12.

6 Fawcett, Jr., *Life, Ministry, and Writings*, 16.

7 Fawcett, Jr., *Life, Ministry, and Writings*, 17.

William Grimshaw and Henry Venn (a founding member of the Clapham sect) were also influential to Fawcett during this time.

While Fawcett ended up becoming a Baptist minister, it is clear there were many significant influences upon him from different denominations, including Puritan writers before him, the Methodists, and the Anglicans. No doubt these influences helped shape his understanding of how Christians ought to overlook theological controversies and differences when necessary. Fawcett, Jr. wrote of Fawcett's spiritual path, "From the whole of this account, what powerful arguments may be drawn for mutual forbearance among professing Christians! It is evident that, in the dispensation of his special favors, the Almighty is 'no respecter of persons,' or of the denominations by which the professors of Christianity are known among men."[8] Fawcett, Jr. concludes from his father's life that God works through many denominations and Christians of different persuasions, and we ought to forbear one another's differences. This background led Fawcett to help his church and others through great times of controversy, especially in the controversy on "high Calvinism." Fawcett, Jr. said "Neither his taste, nor his talents, as before been stated, led him to engage in controversy. He had an utter aversion to it."[9]

Fawcett became a candidate for baptism and church fellowship in a Baptist church in Bradford at the age of nineteen in February 1758 under the ministry of William Crabtree, then married fellow Baptist member Susannah.[10] He remained at this church for six years and began his family, then succeeded Richard Smith as pastor of the Baptist church in Wainsgate in 1765. His theology is expressed in his *Advice to Youth*, written in 1778, where he made clear the free offer of the gospel within a Calvinistic framework, fighting against the hyper-Calvinism that was a great controversy among Christians of his day and showing he was "a Fullerite long before the term was used as one of approbation or of abuse."[11]

As a minister, Fawcett believed that the church had wider responsibilities than to just the local, individual congregation, as he wrote in his contribution to the circular letter, *The Duties and Privileges of Christian Churches*, and he stayed very busy to prove his beliefs. He was involved in planting new churches at Rochdale, Bingley, and Lockwood and wrote a *Constitution of a Gospel Church Considered* (1797) to fight against "the chaotic individualism of the past," according to Sellars.[12] He was involved in the Baptist Missionary Society, founding a branch of the society at Halifax with William Crabtree, and corresponded personally with William Carey in India, collecting money for him.[13] Another area in which Fawcett worked

---

8 Fawcett, Jr., *Life, Ministry, and Writings*, 34.

9 Fawcett, Jr., *Life, Ministry, and Writings*, 107.

10 Fawcett, Jr., *Life, Ministry, and Writings*, 40–41.

11 Ian Sellers, "Other Times, Other Ministries: John Fawcett and Alexander McLaren," *Baptist Quarterly*, 32 (1986–1987): 183.

12 Sellars, "Other Times, Other Ministries," 184.

13 Sellars, "Other Times, Other Ministries," 184.

was training up other ministers. He helped establish the Northern Education Society at Rochdale in 1804 and had a small group of ministerial candidates he was training in his own home.[14] He was introduced to the Clapham Sect by Henry Foster, a friend from youth, and he also had a great interest in caring for the poor, as seen in his tract, *The Attention and Compassion Due to the Children of the Poor* (1808).[15] To help care for poor children, he founded Sunday schools and ran his own private printing press between 1795–1800 and wrote a three-volume *Devotional Family Bible* (1811) for "families in the lower walks of life."[16] Somewhere amidst all his responsibilities, he found time to write hymns for his congregation, many of which have continued to be sung today.

"The passions" in Fawcett's Essay on Anger
Fawcett, like his contemporary Isaac Watts, was concerned with the passions and affections, hence his writing a treatise on anger. His careful use of terminology reflects drawing from the great historical Christian tradition of thinking on the Thomas Dixon's work *From Passions to Emotions: The Creation of a Secular Psychological Category* seeks to explain how the term "passions" was replaced by "emotions" between around 1800–1850 in the general English language and explains what we lose from understanding the passions. Key to Dixon's thesis is that very important different ideas such as passions, affections, and moral sentiments were all lumped into the catch-all term emotions (or in more popular terms, feelings). Writing in the 1780s, Fawcett uses the term "passions" over a hundred times (exclusively in a negative sense), "affections" or "affected" twenty-one times (exclusively in a positive sense) and only using the term "irregular emotions" once (in a negative sense). Christian writing today has sorely lacked an understanding of the history of thought on moral psychology and has given up the traditional categories within the faculties of the soul. Emotions are celebrated and generally seen as positive, as long as we can root out the sinful ones, and experiences such as grief, anger, nervousness, and cheerfulness are all listed as being of the same category.[17]

The new term "emotions" also reflects a different understanding of personhood and theological anthropology that Christians have swallowed as philosophy has changed. Dixon says in the history of philosophy, there was a change from "a

---

14 Sellars, "Other Times, Other Ministries," 184.

15 Sellars, "Other Times, Other Ministries," 184.

16 Sellars, "Other Times, Other Ministries," 183–4.

17 For example, Francis Chan praises all emotions and puts them all in the same category when he says, "In our culture, having feelings or emotions is often equated with weakness. This is a lie that is deeply ingrained in many of us. God created feelings, surely like anything else they can be misused and abused, but the intent and purpose of feelings came from God, since he created emotions. Why is it difficult to believe that he himself has emotions?" Quoted from the Daily Christian Quote, accessed September 6, 2022, https://www.dailychristianquote.com/francis-chan-5/.

realist to a non-realist view of the will" during this time of the change in terms.[18] The Christian view was a realist one, that the will and intellect were the two main faculties of the soul, and the passions and affections were important categories of this active part of the soul.[19] This realist view was held by philosophers and theologians such as Aristotle, Augustine, and Thomas Aquinas, through Descartes and Thomas Reid up until Thomas Brown (1778–1820), who introduced the term "emotions" in a very different explanation of psychology and the will, the non-realist view. This non-realist view said that the "will" was a feeling, and humans experience various involuntary states of "sensations," "emotions," and "thoughts." The realist understanding, rooted in Christian thinking was that the will and intellect were rational and active, whereas the non-realist, which has dominated philosophy since, explained that the will was subject to non-cognitive states and was involuntary. Brown himself claimed there was an important difference in the terms when he said, "A difference of words is, in this case, more than a mere verbal difference. Though it be not the expression of a difference of doctrine, it very speedily becomes so."[20] Because of the shift in terms, Christians today have often unknowingly embraced a more secular, scientific-based understanding of the soul rather than the traditional Christian view, and Fawcett would have been writing in a long historical tradition of understanding the passions and affections, giving great insight to us today on how to understand anger.

Another key term in discussing the passions is affections, which medieval Christian theology developed especially in response to Stoicism. There has long been debate on the relation between Stoicism and Christianity, but Dixon argues that Christians wanted to argue against the Stoics "that some human feeling or affection is proper and necessary to this life, but also that God, the angels and perfected humans are free from the turmoil and perturbations of sin and the passions. This was the heart of Christian affective psychology."[21] For Thomas Aquinas, the passions were physiological and ungodly, whereas the affections were godly acts of the will.[22] There were also proper and improper objects for the passions and affections, such as God versus the world, or eternal life, versus pleasure. These categories continued to be important for Christian theology especially throughout the Puritans, who continued to develop the ideas of the passions and affections.

Key influences for Fawcett's understanding of the passions and affections would have been Jonathan Edwards who wrote his *Treatise Concerning Religious Affections* (1746) and Isaac Watts, who wrote *Discourse of the Love of God and its Influence on*

---

18 Thomas Dixon, *From Passions to Emotions: The Creation of a Secular Psychological Category* (Cambridge, Cambridge University Press, 2006), 250.

19 Dixon, *From Passions to Emotions*, 250.

20 Thomas Brown, *Lectures on the Philosophy of the Human Mind*, Gutenberg.org, accessed September 6, 2022, https://www.gutenberg.org/files/43116/43116-h/43116-h.htm.

21 Dixon, *From Passions to Emotions*, 61.

22 Dixon, *From Passions to Emotions*, 56.

all the Passions (1746) and was the only Christian thinker that Fawcett specifically names and quotes in his *Essay*.[23] Both Edwards and Watts were responding to revivalism, arguing for a balance between a strict formality of religion with emotion and fanaticism that could be seen as unchecked and deceptive. Watts was also quoted as an authority in Samuel Johnson's 1755 dictionary of the English language in his entry on the passions, and Johnson's dictionary is a helpful window into how Fawcett would have been using terms such as "affection," "appetite," "emotion," "feeling," "passion," "sensibility," and "sentiment," all entries in his dictionary.[24]

Fawcett also lived during a time where Christianity was very concerned with correct responses and emotions to religious preaching and teaching. A distinctive aspect of early evangelicalism, according to Tom Schwanda, is the experiential aspect of spirituality and love for God.[25] George Whitefield wrote, "True devotion fills our lives with the greatest peace and happiness that can be enjoyed in his world," reflecting this aspect of early evangelical spirituality.[26] Fawcett's treatise reflects a desire to help Christians with rightly ordered passions and affections, but his hymns also have this focus. In his hymn, "The Christian Awakened," he wrote in the first stanza, "With melting heart and weeping eyes,/My guilty soul for mercy cries;/What shall I do, or whither flee,/T'escape that vengeance due to me?"[27] In a hymn about desire entitled, "Thou Dearest Object of My Love," he writes in the first stanza, "Thou dearest object of my love,/I long to dwell with thee above;/Vain would I leave the world and rise/To yon fair mansion in the skies."[28] Because Fawcett often wrote these hymns to be sung after his sermons, they also show the themes he had been preaching on as well.

Drawing from ancient philosophy
In his essay on anger, Fawcett draws from a number of people in his essay but almost exclusively from the Ancient Greco-Roman philosophical tradition. Excluding Scripture, he draws the most from the Stoic philosopher Seneca, quoting him at least six times. He also quotes or draws from Ancient Greek philosopher Pythagoras (c.570–490 BC), Socrates, Plato, Greek philosopher and student of Aristotle Theophrastus (c.371–281 BC), emperor and student of Stoicism Julius Caesar, the Roman philosopher Cicero (106–43 BC), the Roman philosopher Cato

---

23 Michael Haykin writes that Fawcett would have been reading Edwards by the 1760s and says, "More than any other eighteenth-century author, Edwards showed Sutcliff, and fellow Baptists like Fawcett and Evans, how to combine a commitment to Calvinism with a passion for revival, fervent evangelism and experiential religion" (Haykin, *One Heart and One Soul: John Sutcliff of Olney, his friends, and his times* [Darlington, England: Evangelical Press, 1994], 55).

24 Dixon, *From Passions to Emotions*, 62.

25 Tom Schwanda, *The Emergence of Evangelical Spirituality: The Age of Edwards, Newton, and Whitefield* (New York: Paulist Press, 2016), 8.

26 Schwanda, *Emergence of Evangelical Spirituality*, 8.

27 John Fawcett, "The Christian Awakened."

28 John Fawcett, "Thou Dearest Object of My Love."

(95–46 BC) and the Greek philosopher Plutarch (c.46–119 AD). He quotes or references these philosophers almost always positively, referencing helpful things they wrote, such as, "Let a man (says Seneca) consider his own vices, reflect upon his own follies, and he will see that he has the greatest reason to be angry with himself."[29] He also draws from the Roman poet Horace, the Greek poet Homer, and the modern philosophers John Locke and Francis Hutcheson. On the other hand, he does not quote from Calvin, Baxter, or Edwards, or any other Christian thinkers apart from his contemporary Isaac Watts.

One might wonder what Fawcett's view of secular philosophy was and ask why he draws so much from the ancient Greek and Roman tradition rather than the Christian tradition. First, Fawcett is an example of the Christian humanist tradition of the early modern era where Christians were trained in Greek and Roman philosophy, were conversant with Latin texts, and drew consistently from secular sources. Calvin and others before Fawcett also interacted with the Stoic tradition and other ancient philosophy. It is remarkable though that Fawcett was largely self-educated, began preaching at sixteen, and was the Baptist pastor of a small, poor country church and yet wrote on this scholarly level. Fawcett also shows the limits of secular philosophy and shows where the gospel has to be our ultimate source of comfort and consolation when he says, "Philosophy may infuse fortitude, but religion only gives divine tranquillity in a dying hour."[30]

A second reason Fawcett might have relied heavily on philosophy was that he was very concerned with Christian behavior as a witness to outsiders, and often referenced stories of Christians living contrary to their calling and beliefs, whereas he references positive examples of pagan examples. He says of the Christians, "I cannot wholly suppress, though I am unwilling to enlarge upon, the persecution which the nonconformists, or dissenters from the establishment underwent in *England* for many years."[31] On the other hand, he references examples of Plato, Socrates, and Julius Caesar all showing great moral character in difficult circumstances. "Socrates having without any provocation received a rude blow on his head by an insulting bravado; bore it with that patience which may put Christians to the blush," he says.[32] In another example, he says, "When Julius Caesar was affronted, he repeated the alphabet before he would open his lips to speak on the occasion."[33] Fawcett was concerned with showing Christians that

---

[29] John Fawcett, *An Essay on Anger* (Leeds: Thomas Wright, 1787), 25.

[30] Fawcett, *Essay on Anger*, 102.

[31] Fawcett, *Essay on Anger*, 52. Interestingly, the 1824 edition of Fawcett's essay includes a whole added paragraph, no doubt from the editor and not Fawcett, that says, "In every part of the world has superstition and the lust of power, usurped the name of Christianity to violate its most sacred precepts; the wars of the Cevennes, the burning of Servetus at Geneva, and of the Martyrs in Smithfield, the massacres of heathens by Charlemagne in Saxony, the Huguenots in France, and of the Catholics in Ireland, where the extirpation of the people of a whole province of every age and sex by Cromwell, was perpetrated in the name of the living God" (Reference).

[32] Fawcett, *Essay on Anger*, 116.

[33] Fawcett, *Essay on Anger*, 34.

even the pagans were working hard at putting anger to death. How much worse is a Christian's behavior in having uncontrolled anger when pagans have mastered their passions so well?

Concerned with the home
A unique aspect of Fawcett's essay on anger is that he was concerned with how rampant anger can be within the privacy of the home. Fawcett was a father of several children and dealt with many families in his congregation, knowing how difficult anger can be for those who are raising children: "Few persons meet with more frequent provocations than those who have a number of children to manage and govern."[34] There are multiple sections in his essay where Fawcett addresses how to deal with anger in the home, especially in parenting. This is a uniquely practical part of Fawcett's treatise and an emphasis not even seen in other treatises on anger or even contemporary books on the same topic.

The first time Fawcett discusses how anger comes up in the home is in his chapter on lawful uses of anger, pointing out that there is a kind of anger with sin and disorder that Christians are to have. He acknowledges the difficulty having anger towards the sin in our homes without acting in sin by saying, "To preserve due authority in our families, so as to prevent or suppress disorder, negligence, and vice, without forfeiting our own peace of mind, is, perhaps, in our present state of imperfection, as difficult a branch of duty as any assigned us by providence."[35] This duty of discipline primarily falls to the masculine side of the home as he says, "This cannot be done without manly resolution, constant circumspection, sobriety and gravity."[36] An example he gives is Eli who did not discipline his sons and did not carry out this responsibility and was then punished. The kind of anger that Fawcett is recommending is not a kind of wrath or tyranny. There is a fine line between the sinful kind of anger in authority and a righteous one. He says, "The great secret of family government lies in maintaining authority without moroseness, discipline without tyranny, and resentment of disorder without rash anger; in preserving decorum and regularity without wounding our own peace of mind. The wise and virtuous parent or master is armed with sedate resolution, and a proper firmness of soul."[37] The parent must show a discipline of emotions and use their negative emotions as the psalmist did in hating sin and loving righteousness. He references several verses from the psalms about disciplining one's affections to love good and hate evil in what we gaze at, what our heart yearns for, and what we set before our eyes.

Fawcett then comes back to the theme of domestic peace and happiness in chapter eight, where he gives with rules for the suppression of sinful anger. He

---

34 Fawcett, *Essay on Anger*, 146.

35 Fawcett, *Essay on Anger*, 20.

36 Fawcett, *Essay on Anger*, 20.

37 Fawcett, *Essay on Anger*, 21.

emphasizes how important this peace in homes is and gives directions to husbands, parents, masters, and domestics. He says, "How shocking it is to live a life of tumult and contention in our own families; to have perpetual disquietudes in our own houses, where above all other places we should be concerned to maintain peace! If a man has not peace at home, where can he expect it?"[38] He gives numerous examples from Scripture of both bad and good families: there is the extreme of Eli's indulgence and Nabal's "brutal churlishness," and we should aim to live out Psalm 133:1 among our own families ("How good and pleasant a thing it is for brethren to dwell together in unity!").[39] There are many examples given of husbands or wives who were not helpful to their spouses in pursuing God such as "Socrates had his Xantippe, Abagail her churlish Nabal, Job a wife who tempted him to curse God, Moses a Zipporah, averse to duty, and David a scoffing Michal."[40] There can be so much good done in homes when spouses are helpful to each other in following God and maintaining a brotherly fellowship among all the household.

Concerned with Christian unity
Fawcett's famous hymn, "Blest Be the Tie That Binds," is indicative of his strong concern and desire for Christian unity, but he also reflected and shaped early evangelicalism in wanting more flexibility among Christians to overlook tertiary doctrinal matters such as forms of church government and this concern is also a central one in the essay. According to Mark Noll, one of key tenets of early evangelicalism was a flexibility of being able to work amongst Christians of different denominations. George Whitefield was an example of this, who would be criticized for allowing a Baptist minister to take part in a communion service, or preached alongside the Presbyterian revivalist Gilbert Tennent, but Whitefield responded, "It was best to preach the new birth, and the power of godliness, and not to insist so much on the form: for people would never be brought to one mind as to that; nor did Jesus Christ ever intend it."[41] This example and statement of Whitefield's was no doubt influential to Fawcett's approach to ministry, and Fawcett's concern that Christians fight anger is especially that we fight against unnecessary division among Christians.

In chapter four, Fawcett lists nine ways we sin in our anger, one of them being focusing on the anger involved in divisions among Christians: We sin "when we are angry with those who differ from us in religious sentiments."[42] He says that Christ commanded Christians to "search the Scriptures" and "to call no man master on

---

38 Fawcett, *Essay on Anger*, 81.

39 Fawcett, *Essay on Anger*, 79.

40 Fawcett, *Essay on Anger*, 82.

41 Mark Noll, *The Rise of Evangelicalism: The Age of Edwards, Whitefield and the Wesleys* (Downers Grove, IL: Intervarsity Press, 2003), 15.

42 Fawcett, *Essay on Anger*, 46.

earth," giving them the liberty or private judgment.[43] He says, "Let us not therefore thunder our anathemas against those who may differ from us in some points of doctrine of branches of worship; neither let us pass angry censures upon them. Let us remember that meekness and love are essential to Christianity."[44] Practically speaking, Fawcett points out a number of reasons why we might differ on points of doctrine. We have different backgrounds of education and differences in who or what influenced and taught us early on in our Christianity which leads to partiality or prejudice in what we might believe.[45] We should remember there are wise and good men involved on all sides of debate and treasure meekness and modesty so to not become too confident in our own opinions. We should not believe that "we were the people, and wisdom should die with us" (referencing Job 12:2).[46]

The expulsive power of cheerfulness and friendship
Fawcett says he thinks the most valuable part of his essay is his spelling out how the greatest antidote to anger is cheerfulness. Christian cheer is another theme throughout the essay, referenced at least twenty-four times. He contrasts cheerfulness with mirth by saying that mirth is "short and transient" and subject to the ups and downs of melancholy. Mirth is only an act, whereas cheerfulness is "a habit of mind," and is more "fixed and permanent" and prevents the severe ups and downs that mirth can bring about.[47]

Fawcett says we should develop cheerfulness in three aspects: with ourselves (in our thoughts), with others, and with our great Author. The person who focuses on developing cheerfulness in his mind is "a perfect master of all the powers and faculties of the soul; his imagination is clear, and his judgment undisturbed; his temper is even and unruffled, whether in action or in solitude."[48] This inward mastery over the faculties is similar to the Stoic tradition, but rather than seeking *apatheia* (being free of all passions) in Stoicism, Fawcett presents the emphasis and goal as being able to "relish to all those goods which nature has provided for him, tastes all the pleasures of the creation which are poured forth about him."[49] Cheerfulness, gratitude, and being able to enjoy God's creation is Fawcett's emphasis rather than simply the lack of passions.

In relation to others, cheerfulness ought to spill out into our influence on others. It can be seen in good humor and in a kind of "sudden sunshine" that affects others. This cheerfulness is especially important for friendships, which was very

---

43 Fawcett, *Essay on Anger*, 47.

44 Fawcett, *Essay on Anger*, 47.

45 Fawcett, *Essay on Anger*, 50.

46 Fawcett, *Essay on Anger*, 51.

47 Fawcett, *Essay on Anger*, 146.

48 Fawcett, *Essay on Anger*, 147.

49 Fawcett, *Essay on Anger*, 147.

important for the early evangelical ministers such as Fawcett, Fuller, Whitefield, and the Wesleys. Michael Haykin brings this out in his book on Fuller who especially cultivated and maintained friendships with Christians such as Samuel Pearce and John Ryland and rebuked the Scottish Baptists for being too divisive.[50] Fawcett, a friend of Fuller's, also reflected this desire for Christian unity and said, "The heart rejoices of its own accord, and naturally flows out into friendship and benevolence towards the person who has so kind an effect upon it."[51] Friendship was a key way to develop one's spirituality and fight anger. In the way he ends his essay, he signals that a main reason for writing his essay on anger was to combat the anger involved in being overly divisive in the Christian church and in being too quick to separate oneself from other Christians. He says at the end, "May we, by putting on the Lord Jesus Christ, and learning of him to be meek and lowly in heart, be formed to a meekness for, and finally by his saving mercy be brought to the possession of, the regions of perfect peace and purity, where friendship, harmony, and love flourish and reign through immortal ages! Amen."[52]

Conclusion

In this paper, I have sought to show how John Fawcett's life as a pastor is a great example of Christian faithfulness and living out a desire for peace and unity within the church. His essay on anger gives insight on how we are to live out harmonious living among sinful Christians by putting anger to death in very specific ways. He also gives many insights on how we are to do this in our homes and practice gentleness and peace among those we interact with the most in home. A main way we can gain from Fawcett's work is how we should be wary of our anger among other Christians. Fawcett and the early evangelicals valued friendship, unity, and brotherhood and saw anger as a danger to these precious treasures. So much of Fawcett's words on anger could be applied to the dangers of internet theology and disputes over tertiary matters. The internet and other modern forms of technology especially can mask anger and make us think we are not acting in anger, whereas many of the words written on the internet are filled of anger, missed priorities, or bad timing. Anger is not excused when it is written out online rather than spoken face to face, even though many of us can forget this when shielded behind a screen. As Fawcett puts it, "In all our religious connections and concerns especially, let us wear the garment of humility, and the ornaments of a meek and quiet spirit. This will be more to the honor of our Divine Savior, more to the credit of our holy religion, than the exactest orthodoxy in doubtful matters without it."[53]

---

50 Michael A.G. Haykin, *The armies of the Lamb: The spirituality of Andrew Fuller* (Dundas, ON: Joshua Press, 2001), 42–46.

51 Fawcett, *Essay on Anger*, 147.

52 Fawcett, *Essay on Anger*, 150.

53 Fawcett, *Essay on Anger*, 139.

Texts & documents

"Clipston Revival—July 10th 1800: An account & remarks of the revival in the congregation at Clipston derived from the Church Records"[1]

ed. Sean Carter

Introduction
In 1792, the leadership of Clipston Baptist Church reported how that Sutcliff's reprint of Jonathan Edwards' *Humble Attempt* had been a tremendous encouragement to them in the whole matter of praying for revival. The congregation decided to set aside February 25, 1795 in particular for prayer and fasting for revival in their locality.

Text
Last year was most remarkable for the church. Zeal and service for God had declined. Everybody was dejected and dismayed. There was so much deadness, carnality and inattention that many of us were greatly discouraged, fearing our usefulness was finished.

Often some of us would talk about the unpromising state of the congregation and lament to see so little fruit arising from our labours. It was particularly affecting to behold the spirit and conduct of the youth. Many were brought up in church the children of pious parents. They attended church but were unimpressed, untouched and indifferent. Some were trifling and indecent in behaviour at church and disrespectful and rude.

The minister gave an annual address to them every year. However, their profligacy and profanity amidst so many ineffectual works for their spiritual improvement so disheartened him he could not face speaking to them. Such was

---

1 Original found in "Miscellanea Edintone: a collection of items mostly on nonconformity and Northamptonshire," https://edintone.com/centre-for-the-nations/clipston-revival/. Used by permission of Graham Ward.

the state of things amongst us we were sinking into deep despondency. Amidst all these discouragements however, there were those amongst us whose hearts trembled for the work of God, were fervent in prayer and joined in endeavours to promote the interests of true religion. We frequently set apart days for solemn prayer by the whole church, these times bought refreshment and comfort amidst our bondage. At such times we hoped we should live to see better days, and greater things than these.

During January 1800, one young man, John Gulliver, had for some time been under religious impressions, was now awakened by a deep sense of religion by the death of his mother.

He became serious and fervent and stirred up others to a great diligence and fervency in the ways of God. Our monthly prayer meetings attendance grew, the conversation at those meetings was how to promote religion, the general state of the churches at home and abroad, and sharing what God was doing elsewhere. The attendance at prayer grew.

Two or three young people attending these meetings wanted to pray more often, they started a prayer meeting among themselves. Soon after these meetings began, accounts were received of revival happening elsewhere. This news caused the sparks which had been kindled in the bosom of a few to burst into a flame which spread from heart to heart.

The young people meeting for prayer now increased and outgrew the meeting place so they met elsewhere. They then began to meet every evening, the meeting became so well attended they started to meet in the church building.

It was very common with the young people to have several meetings of a more private nature. Late in the evenings after coming from public worship half a dozen of them will retire to one friend's house and half a dozen to another for the purpose of sharing their thoughts and feelings more freely. Some times a few of them have met together in the vestry to pray at four o'clock in the morning for mutual prayer. At noon hour some of them retire into the fields and spend a little time in prayer and spiritual conversation before they return to the labours of the day.

We had not really rejoiced over this work due to our fears as to whether or not it was genuinely of God and many of the impressions false. However, we have had time for observation and have concluded that the work is of God. The work has not been accompanied by noise and excitement but with repentance and prayers.

Meeting for prayer was the cause of this revival more than preaching. Preaching however has led many to inquire about the way of salvation. The youth Invited others to church meetings and many who came were deeply touched. In tears and weeping they have sought the way to Zion.

This work has effected a change among the youth in Clipston. Their behaviour is now mild and gentle. The streets during summer evenings were thronged with misbehaving idle youth, now they are silent and still. They walk together in groups praying and talking about religion.

The effect is mainly among the youth.

The Clipston congregation experienced considerable growth averaging 700–800 people in a service.

In 1803 a new church building was commissioned.

A Newly Discovered Letter from John Ryland, Jr. (1753–1825) to Christopher Anderson (1782–1852)

Edited Baiyu Andrew Song

Baiyu Andrew Song (PhD, FRAS) is a research associate and teaching fellow at the Andrew Fuller Centre for Baptist Studies, Cambridge, Ontario. He is also an adjunct professor at Carey Theological College, Vancouver, and at Redeemer University, Ancaster.

Introduction
Manuscripts are necessary for students of history. Too often, historians lament the lack of primary sources and documentary evidence. For that reason, Edward William Hooker (1794-1875), a descendent of Thomas Hooker (1686–1647), emphasised the importance "of the careful and conscientious preservation and deposit in safe keeping, under the auspices of some society, of all manuscript and other papers, which may afford materials for future preparation of histories or lives."[1] Furthermore, the discovery and preservation of manuscripts should not be left to accident, or the antiquarians; instead, "every member of a historical society may probably consider himself as a member of a committee of research, on its behalf; who shall live with his eyes open and his thoughts on the alter in reference to this object."[2] Among Baptists, a few of such history-minded collectors and preservers should be remembered, men such as Isaac Mann (1785–1831), who "kept an extensive epistolary correspondence," and C.B. Jewson (1909–1981), former Lord Mayor of Norwich.[3] Nevertheless, it is equally important to emphasize the accessibility of the manuscripts. In other words, purchased manuscripts should

---

[1] Edward William Hooker, "The Preservation of Manuscripts," *New England Historical and Genealogical Register* 17 (July 1863): 269.

[2] Hooker, "The Preservation of Manuscripts," 270.

[3] William Steadman, "A Brief Memoir of the Late Rev. Isaac Mann, A.M.," *Baptist Magazine* 7 (February 1832): 47. On a calendar of letters collected by Mann, see F.G. Hastings and W.T. Whitley, ed., "Calendar of Letters, 1742-1831," *Baptist Quarterly* 6.1 (1932): 39–43; *Baptist Quarterly*, 6.4 (1932): 173–186; *Baptist Quarterly*, 6.7 (1933): 318–322; *Baptist Quarterly*, 6.8 (1933): 373–379; *Baptist Quarterly*, 7.1 (1934): 39–46; *Baptist Quarterly*, 7.2 (1934): 89–91; *Baptist Quarterly*, 7.3 (1934): 138–139; *Baptist Quarterly*, 7.4 (1935): 175–185; *Baptist Quarterly*, 7.5 (1935): 235–238. Also see T. Crist, "Isaac Mann's Collection of Letters," *Baptist Quarterly* 26.3 (1975): 134–139.

not be locked in personal libraries; instead, buyers––even churches––need to either donate or permanently loan the manuscript to an archive for public access. Too many manuscripts have been lost or destroyed in personal belongings and even in the hands of "Whiggish" church leaders. Historians, thus, bear a moral responsibility for discovering and preserving manuscripts.

The following text became available for sale in the spring of 2023. Soon after discovering it, I purchased this manuscript in March 2023. During one of my trips to England, I donated it as a permanent loan to the Angus Library and Archives at Regent's Park College, Oxford. At its new home, the document is renamed as "John Ryland junior Letter," with "D/RYS" as its call number. I am grateful to Emily Borgoyne, the Librarian, for arranging and facilitating the loan. Since I technically own its copyright, it is appropriate to announce this newly discovered letter from John Ryland, Jr. to Christopher Anderson, dated November 1816, in the *Journal of Andrew Fuller Studies*.

Authorship, Recipient, and Date
Based on the signature and calligraphy, it is patent that this short letter was written by John Ryland, Jr., then pastor of Broadmead Baptist Chapel, Bristol, and principal of the Bristol Academy. Since Andrew Fuller's (1754–1815) death, Ryland also served as the Baptist Missionary Society's interim co-secretary with James Hinton (1761–1823). Later, he was assisted by John Dyer (1783–1841).[4] Ryland addressed his recipient as "my dear brother" in the letter, and the rear side of the letter shows that its recipient was "Rev^d. C. Anderson" of "Edinburgh." The latter, of course, is Christopher Anderson of Edinburgh, who is mentioned in the October 1815 minutes of the Baptist Missionary Society (BMS) General Committee's minute, which was penned by Ryland. In both cases, the "c" is outstandingly large, especially in contrast to the following letter "a."[5] Furthermore, since Christopher Anderson's initial application to become a missionary in 1804 and his study trip to England in 1805, he was well-known to Ryland, and had even studied at the Bristol Academy.[6]

---

[4] F.A. Cox, *History of the Baptist Missionary Society, from 1792 to 1842* (London: T. Ward & Co., and G. & J. Dyer, 1842), 2:270–274.

[5] On October 10, 1815, the general committee met in the vestry of College Lane chapel, Northampton, and it was resolved that "the cordial thanks of this Society be presented to the Rev^d. Christopher Anderson, of Edinburgh, for the many important services, which he has render'd, in various ways, to the Society, & that he also be requested to continue them" ("An Account of the Proceedings of the Baptist Missionary Society. Since the Vote Passed at Luton, May 16, 1815 desiring J. Ryland of Bristol to act as Secretary pro tempore," Acc No 4 Gen/CTTEE 4 Micro 1 [Shelf xxv/1] [Angus Library and Archive, Regent's Park College, Oxford], 9).

[6] Hugh Anderson, *The Life and Letters of Christopher Anderson* (Edinburgh: William P. Kennedy; London: Hamilton, Adams, and Co.; Dublin: J. McGlashan, 1854), 34. In fact, in a letter to John Saffery (1763–1825), Ryland stated his desire for Christopher Anderson to become the new BMS secretary: "I think Anderson w^d. do the best of any one of whom I can think, but fear we shall be unable to bring him in" (John Ryland, Jr. to John Saffery, May 22, 1815, D/MRC 8/32 [Angus Library and Archive, Regent's Park College, Oxford], 2). As Brian Stanley pointed out, Robert Hall's (1764–1831) opposition to Anderson's secretaryship was deeply rooted, as Hall feared that Anderson would carry out Fuller's close-communion policy. Furthermore, quoting A.C. Underwood (b. 1885), Stanley agrees that with Anderson's advocacy for the missionaries, the Serampore controversy could have been prevented if Anderson had become the secretary (Brian Stanley, *The His-*

From that point on, Ryland and Anderson had regularly corresponded with each other.[7] In light of Ryland's Scottish trip in July 1816, and the publication of his memoir of Andrew Fuller in late July 1816, it was not unusual for Christopher Anderson to request a copy of Ryland's memoir in a following letter.[8]

Another issue is the date of the letter. Though the letter contains no date, the postal stamps can provide some hints. The first stamp indicates that the letter and its attached parcel were sent from Bristol on November 25, 1816. The second stamp shows that the letter-parcel left Birmingham on November 29, 1816, but it is unknown when the letter-parcel was delivered to Anderson. The letter can be dated to around but not later than November 25, 1816.

Content

At first sight, this letter appears to contain insignificant information; a closer examination, however, reveals this brief letter's historical value. Besides the rareness of Ryland's manuscript letters, this letter also adds nuance to Ryland's close relationship with Christopher Anderson.[9] In Anderson's memoir by his nephew, there are extracts of Ryland's letters, dated from December 22, 1815, to July 6, 1816.[10] One of the primary concerns of these extracts was Andrew Fuller's

tory of the Baptist Missionary Society 1792–1992 [Edinburgh: T&T Clark, 1992], 33, 34).

7 See Anderson, *Life and Letters of Christopher Anderson*, 181–253.

8 Ryland was accompanied by John Saffery and John Dyer and visited Scotland in July 1816 on behalf of the Baptist Missionary Society (BMS). However, the trip is not in the society's general committee minutes. Nevertheless, the *Caledonian Mercury*, a Scottish newspaper, recorded on July 25, 1816, that Ryland, Saffery, and Dyer "are expected to arrive in Edinburgh this evening." It further reported the visitors' itinerary as "Thursday, this evening, the 25th, at half past six o'clock, Dr Ryland or Mr Saffery will preach at Dalkeith, in the Rev. Thomas Brown's Meeting-house; and this evening, at seven, Mr Dyer will preach in Richmond Court Chapel. On Friday evening, the Ministers will attend the General Meeting of the Edinburgh Auxiliary Missionary Society in the Rev. Mr Smith's Chapel, College Street. Next Lord's day, Dr Ryland will preach in Mr Innes's place, Elder Street, in the forenoon; in the afternoon in Mr Anderson's, Richmond Court; and in the evening, at half past six, in the Rev. Mr Peddie's Meeting-house, Bristo Street. Mr Saffery, of Salisbury, will preach in the forenoon in Richmond Court Chapel, in the afternoon the Elder Street, and in the evening in Mr Aikman's Chapel, Argyll Street. Collections will be made at each of these places of worship. These at Mr Anderson's and Mr Innes's are in aid of the Mission Stations, and the others are in aid of the Oriental Translations. Dr Ryland will proceed by Handington and Berwick to England, and Mess. Saffery and Dyer go to the North as far as Inverness; but these places will be more particularly noticed in our next paper" ("To the Friends of Christianity in Scotland," *Caledonian Mercury* 14768 [July 25, 1816]: 3).

According to the *Eclectic Review*, the *New Evangelical Magazine*, and the *Baptist Magazine*, Ryland's memoir was probably published by the end of July 1816, as the editor of the former noticed that "Dr. John Ryland proposes to publish an edition of the Works of the late Rev. Andrew Fuller, including several new MSS. And a Memoir of the Author, in nine or ten octavo volumes" ("Art. XVI. Select Literary Information," *Eclectic Review* 6 [July 1816]: 101). The *New Evangelical Magazine* noticed in July 1816 that "the work of Faith, the labour of Love, and the Patience of Hope illustrated, in the Life and Death of the Rev. Andrew Fuller, late Pastor of the Baptist church at Kettering, and Secretary to the Baptist Missionary. Chiefly extracted from his own papers by John Ryland, D.D. about 600 pages, 12s. boards" ("New Publications," *New Evangelical Magazine, and Theological Review* 2 [July 1816]: 223). Similarly, the editor of the *Baptist Magazine* also noticed the publication of Ryland's memoir in July 1816 ("Lately Published," *Baptist Magazine* 8 [July 1816]: 297). However, reviews did not appear until in 1818 when Ryland issued the second edition of his memoir.

9 For a list of Ryland's manuscript letters, see Lon Graham, *All Who Love Our Blessed Redeemer: The Catholicity of John Ryland Jr.* (Eugene, OR: Pickwick, 2022), 189–190.

10 Anderson, *Life and Letters of Christopher Anderson*, 246–248.

missiological legacy. Anderson's nephew then quoted Ryland's letter dated June 10, 1817, as if there had been no correspondence between Bristol and Edinburgh for over a year. Thus, the present letter addresses the omission and uncovers some of Ryland's works and thoughts during this time. Despite the holes caused by paper decay, this letter can be divided into three parts concerning Fuller's memoir, the Baptist mission, and domestic news.

As Fuller's designated funeral-sermon preacher and close friend, John Ryland was encouraged by both his widow Ann Coles (1763–1825) and many friends to write a biography of Fuller.[11] As he began to select, transcribe, and edit his friend's papers, Ryland saw his memoir as a part of Fuller's collected works.[12] Furthermore, Ryland believed that

> a faithful retelling of Fuller's life would satisfy public interest and bring a measure of financial support to his surviving family, he was also convinced that "my highest ambition is, like the biographer of David Brainerd [1718–1747], to show what manner of man my friend was, and to excite others to follow him, so far as he followed Christ."[13]

Ryland's memoir was printed by Fuller's son J.G. Fuller (1799–1884) in Kettering and sold by William Button (1754–1821) in London.[14] It is hard to know how many copies were initially printed and sold. As Ryland explained in the prefatory postscript to the second edition of the memoir, "a smaller type has been used, for the sake of reducing the price."[15] Thus, it explains why Ryland only had two copies of Fuller's memoir, and why he hesitated to send a copy to Anderson, despite the demand from his other Scottish connections.

Regarding the Baptist Missionary Society, Ryland indicated that he was busy compiling the thirtieth issue of the *Periodical Accounts*, which recorded various missionary updates from January to June 1815. Ryland then mentioned J.G.

---

11 See Christopher Ryan Griffith, "Editor's Introduction," in *The Life of Andrew Fuller: A Critical Edition of John Ryland's Biography*, ed. Griffith, The Complete Works of Andrew Fuller, vol. 17 (Berlin: de Gruyter, 2021), 11–14.

12 In the *Baptist Magazine*, it was noticed that "Proposals are issued, by Mr. J.G. Fuller, of Kettering, for publishing a complete edition of the works of the late Mr. Andrew Fuller, to be completed in about ten octavo volumes; not to exceed to subscribers, five pounds. Names of subscribes will be received by the Rev. Dr. [John] Ryland, of Bristol; the Rev. Mr. [James] Hinton, of Oxford; the Rev. Mr. [Joseph] Ivimey, of London; or by any of the ministers who belong to the committee of the Baptist Missionary Society. Also, by Mr. Burls, Lothbury; and Gardiner and Son, Book-sellers, princes-street, Cavendish-sq." ("Literary Intelligence," *Baptist Magazine* [December 1815]: 518).

13 Griffith, "Editor's Introduction," 15–16.

14 On the printing and publishing industry, see John Feather, *A History of British Publishing* (London: Croom Helm, 1988); *item*, *The Provincial Book Trade in Eighteenth-Century England* (Cambridge: Cambridge University Press, 1985); James Raven, *The Business of Books: Booksellers and the English Book Trade 1450–1850* (New Haven, CT: Yale University Press, 2007); *item*, *Publishing Business in Eighteenth-Century England* (Woodbridge, Suffolk: Boydell, 2014).

15 John Ryland, Jr., *The Work of Faith, the Labour of Love, and the Patience of Hope, Illustrated; in the Life and Death of the Rev. Andrew Fuller, Late Pastor of the Baptist Church at Kettering, and Secretary to the Baptist Missionary Society, from Its Commencement, in 1792*, 2nd ed. (London: Button & Son, 1818), xvi.

Fuller's removal to Bristol from Kettering. It is curious to ponder the younger Fuller's choice, for, since his father's death, the BMS headquarters had relocated to London. As John Feather pointed out, despite the limitations that provincial printers faced, "the dissenters were more content with provincial publications," whereas Anglican clergymen sought printers in London and the universities.[16] Furthermore, since Bristol was increasingly developed as a major commercial port, along with Southampton, both international and domestic trades enabled increasing work opportunities. As the new printer for the BMS' journal, Fuller's printing skill was praised by William Newman (1773–1835), who told John Sutcliff (1752–1814) on November 27, 1813, that "The last No. of Period. Accts is very interesting and it is excellently printed."[17] Moreover, Fuller also brought with him two young apprentices, Thomas (1799–1824) and William Knibb (1803–1845). As Fuller attended the Broadmead congregation, the Knibb brothers also joined their master and attended Sunday schools, where both were impressed by the missionary work and experienced conversion.[18]

Regarding the demand for missionary updates, Ryland briefly mentioned the conversion of Kiaba (b. c.1788/9), a Bhutanese believer living in Patna, who was first introduced by a Sheemuni-misser to John Thomas Thompson (d. 1850) on November 21, 1814, and received baptism on April 4, 1815. J.T. Thompson, an India-born Eurasian, who worked in the Military Auditor General's Office, was first recognised as a missionary by William Ward (1769–1823) at Serampore in around 1810. He was then sent to Patna, an ancient city more than 500 kilometres northwest of Calcutta, in 1812.[19] Thompson first reported about Kiaba to Ward on

---

16 Feather, *Provincial Book Trade in Eighteenth-Century England*, 118.

17 Timothy D. Whelan, ed., *Baptist Autographs in the John Rylands University Library of Manchester 1741–1845* (Macon, GA: Mercer University Press, 2009), 170.

18 "One Sunday afternoon, before dismissing the children, Mr. [J.G.] Fuller spoke for a few moments from the text [Jeremiah 3:4]. Mr. Fuller aimed at the scholars, but his words smote the conscience and won the heart of a teacher, and that teacher one of his own apprentices! 'It was a moment earnest and affectionate address,' wrote William Knibb, shortly afterwards, 'and, under the divine blessing, it made a deep and, I trust, a lasting impression on my mind, and I hope that I was enabled to cast myself at the foot of the Cross as a perishing sinner, pleading for mercy for the sake of Jesus Christ and for His sake alone!' A day or two later the youth sought an interview with his employer. 'I felt ashamed,' said Knibb, in the course of this conversation with Mr. Fuller, 'I felt ashamed, being a teacher, that the address should be as suitable to me as to the children. I felt conscious that I had wandered as far from God as ever they had, and that I needed a forgiving Father and a constant guide as much as they did. I was over whelmed. I felt such a mixture of shame and grief, of hope and love, as I had never felt before and cannot now describe. I could not join in the closing hymn. I went to my room above and yielded to my feelings. I wept bitterly the text itself into a prayer. 'My Father,' I cried to God, 'wilt not Thou from this time be the guide of my youth?' The Lord heard my prayer and enabled me to give Him my heart; and now it is my earnest desire to yield myself to His guidance as long as I live!' 'O need a forgiving Father!' 'I needed a constant Guide!' 'My Father, wilt not Thou be the guide of my youth?' 'The Lord heard my prayer!' the apprentice says exultingly, as he looks gratefully into his employer's face. And when the Lord heard that prayer, He heard the bitter cry of the island whose fair shores we just now visited; for the salvation of William Knibb was the deliverance of the slaves across the seas'" (F.W. Boreham, *A Bunch of Everlastings or Texts That Made History* [New York: Abingdon, 1920], 214–215).

19 "Particulars of the late Fire at Serampore, and the State of the Mission, collected from the late Accounts of the Missionaries," *Periodical Accounts* 4.23 (1812): 468. Thompson went to Patna with his wife, mother, John D'Silvia, and Rozia D'Rozario. He was ordained on April 25, 1812 (*Periodical Accounts* 5.25 [1813]: 21). Later in 1857, Thompson's widow and

February 2, 1815, and described the young man as "a teachable disposition, very liberal and compassionate to the poor."[20] Kiaba expressed interests to be educated in the Christian faith and "very much to learn to read" the New Testament in Hindi.[21] Thompson began with teaching Kiaba to read in Hindi and reported how the latter began to know the Christian faith:

> On December 1, 1814, I wrote out for him the [Devanagari] alphabet; and after diligent application to reading and writing the characters, he in ten or twelve days began reading a little in the large [Hindi] testament: but as he could not understand what he read in it, for want of the language, (being only twelve months from [Bhutan],) I commenced a small general vocabulary for him, inserting first such words as he knew, and then placing opposite to them the synonymas: this method has happily succeeded, and by it he learns with greater facility and accuracy than he could have done by mere hearing: this vocabulary he commits to memory. He intended to go through the new testament, but when he concluded Matthew's Gospel, he said he would read it over again, as he derived very little satisfaction the first time: accordingly he went over it a second time, and frequently mentioned to me what he had read: he is reading over Matthew the third time, and is now in chapter xxi. To enable him to understand the New Testament the better, I give him, in morning conversations the history of the Old Testament. He partakes of our food, and sleeps in my writing room; reads his testament and vocabulary alternately an hour or so before worship, three hours till dinner, half an hour before we walk out, and from after tea till nine or ten at night. When he first came to us, we found it exceedingly difficult to convey the most general ideas of Christianity, both on account of his being dull of apprehension, and very deficient in the [Hindi] language; the last owing to his habit of speaking his own language with the Cashmerian whom he accompanied from [Bhutan]. I am inserting all the [Bhutanese] words, (in [Hindi] characters,) that I can obtain from Kiaba, in a little book ... Kiaba is very diffident, so that I cannot get him to pray in my hearing: however, from his conversation we hope he is sitting at the feet of Jesus. He said one evening, and wrote it in [Hindi], that Jesus Christ had given Kiaba power to become one of the sons of God. I asked what made him think so; he replied, "Because he has enabled me to read and understand his word in a foreign tongue." I said, there were numbers of persons who did that, and yet they were not the sons of God. He answered, "They do not love the Lord more than their devtas, their peers, and prophets; and they do not trust in the sacrifice of Christ for pardon and salvation; but offer other sacrifices. I now feel in my heart a little love to Christ,

---

two daughters were murdered during the Rebellion of 1857. Thompson was transferred to Delhi in 1817, where he worked till his death. As a result of the Serampore Controversy, Thompson's mission fell under the management of the BMS.

20 "(10) Patna," *Periodical Accounts*, 23.

21 "(10) Patna," *Periodical Accounts*, 28.

and great fear and hatred of the [Hindu] and [Islamic] ways, and of all my native ways: I believe this book to be God's book, and wish to obey his commands. I wish to be baptized in water." It was long before he understood aright the plan of salvation. He now trusts in the death of Christ, but was before inclined to trust in baptism. When I had been speaking of the enmity and wickedness of the Jews towards the Redeemer, he observed, that they did not know him to be God their Saviour, become incarnate. When he saw Europeans going along the streets, be supposed they were distributing the words of salvation, but when informed to the contrary, he said, "They do not know Christ."[22]

Thompson recorded in his journal that a small church meeting was held on April 4, 1815, and it was resolved to receive Kiaba into the church. On the same day, they walked to the riverside with some Roman Catholics, where, "after singing the [Hindi] hymn, 'Jesus, and shalt it ever be, &c.,'" Thompson addressed the crowds and baptised Kiaba in the Ganges River.[23] Thompson was moved emotionally, as he recorded that "when I gave Brother Kiaba the right hand of fellowship, my soul was drawn forth, and I wept, while with trembling joy and a faltering voice, I owned him as our brother in the gospel."[24] They then celebrated the eucharist around three o'clock in the afternoon. After his baptism, Kiaba often accompanied Thompson to preach and distribute books. From their first encounter to Kiaba's baptism, it was less than five months, and curiously, Kiaba's name was never mentioned again in the accounts after 1815. Thus, it seems reasonable for Ryland to complain about the speediness of Kiaba's baptism.

In the last section of his letter, Ryland shared with Anderson some domestic news, among which the conversion of John Edmonds Stock (1774–1835), a Clifton physician, needs to be highlighted. Dr. Stock's father, John Stock (d. 1788), had been a member of the Broadmead congregation since July 10, 1741, and was established as a paper-maker and stationer in Bristol.[25] John Edmonds Stock entered Lincoln's Inn to pursue a legal career on November 9, 1790, but he left within a year and matriculated at Exeter College, Oxford, on March 10, 1791. While at the university, Stock embraced Socinianism and left without taking any degree. He then went to Edinburgh and became a medical student on November 14, 1793. While at Edinburgh, Stock became active in political reforms. With an inflammatory circular letter, Stock and his colleagues were indicted for high treason. Unlike his friends, who were hanged and quartered, Stock managed to escape to Philadelphia. He

---

22 "(10) Patna," *Periodical Accounts*, 23–24.

23 "(10) Patna," *Periodical Accounts*, 30.

24 "(10) Patna," *Periodical Accounts*, 30.

25 "Members' Roll 1734 to 1774," 30251/BD/R/1/3 (Bristol Archives), [3]. Most of the biographical information about Stock are based on Hugh Torrens, "Appendix 1. The mystery of Dr. John Edmonds Stock, Beddoes' first biographer," in *The Enlightenment of Thomas Beddoes: Science, Medicine, and Reform*, ed. Trevor Levere, Larry Stewart, Hugh Torrens, and Joseph Wachelder (London: Routledge, 2017), 238–248.

resumed his medical studies at the University of Pennsylvania and graduated with the degree of MD on May 12, 1797. While in exile, his friend John Edye (1789–1873) sought pardon for Stock, and he finally returned to England in 1803. In the same year, Stock was admitted as an Extra-Licentiate to the College of Physicians of London. He was then elected to the Bristol Royal Infirmary as a physician on March 28, 1811. While being a manager of the Unitarian connexion in Bristol, Stock experienced a change of mind while treating John Vernon (1785–1817), Baptist pastor at Downend, in July 1816.

John Vernon was born at Pailton, near Coventry, on April 15, 1785, to George Varnam (later Vernon, 1740–1820). After his early education, Vernon went to Birmingham for retail trade, and he regularly went to listen to Samuel Pearce (1766–1799) and Jehoiada Brewer (c.1752–1817).[26] In 1805, Vernon went to visit his sister Hephzibah Vernon (d. 1849), who at the time moved to Yarmouth with her husband William Walford (1773–1850), the Congregationalist minister and author of "Sweet Hour of Prayer." Vernon then attended St. Mary's Baptist Chapel in Norwich. After he made a public confession of faith, Vernon was baptised by Joseph Kinghorn (1766–1832) on September 6, 1806. A year later, he entered the Bristol Academy for pastoral training. However, due to ill health, his studies were interrupted. Vernon was ordained as the pastor of Downend Baptist chapel on July 1, 1814. Two years later, Vernon was again seriously ill while visiting a friend in Bristol. For about seven months, Stock visited Vernon once a week, and according to the doctor, Vernon "felt it a duty to endeavour to lead me to reconsider my religious opinions; and at length, with much delicacy and timidity, led to the subject."[27] Stock then took Vernon's advice to consider the Trinitarian arguments seriously. By examining both Socinian and Trinitarian authors, Stock came to the conviction in the last week of October 1816 that "my mind unhesitatingly and thankfully accepted the doctrines of the Supreme Divinity of our Lord and Saviour Jesus Christ; of Atonement or Reconciliation by his precious blood; and of the Divinity and Personality of the Holy Spirit."[28]

Subsequently, Stock wrote a long letter to John Rowe (1764–1832), the Unitarian minister at Lewin's Mead Chapel, expressing his resignation and renouncing Socinianism as untenable. "Dr. Stock's Conversion"--as it was called--soon became a trending local news item and ignited a series of pamphlet wars. After his conversion, Stock attended Downend chapel, where John Foster (1770–1843) ministered from 1817 to 1821. One author noticed that Stock's "religious views underwent no change after the publication of his Letter. He retained full possession of his faculties to the last: but, towards the close of life, his constitution was sadly

---

26 See "Memoir of the Rev. John Vernon, Late Pastor of the Baptist Church at Down-End, Near Bristol," *Baptist Magazine* 9 (June 1817): 201–208; John Ryland, Jr., "CXIV. Salvation by Grace," in *Pastoral Memorials: Selected from the Manuscripts of the late Revd. John Ryland, D.D. of Bristol* (London: B.J. Holdsworth, 1828), 2:125–139.

27 [John Edmonds Stock,] *Correspondence Relative to Unitarianism. Dr. Stock to the Rev. John Rowe; and Dr. Carpenter to the Editor of the Bristol Mirror*, 2nd ed. (Bristol: Browne and Manchee, 1817), 6.

28 [Stock,] *Correspondence Relative to Unitarianism*, 9.

debilitated by several severe attacks of illness," and he died on October 4, 1835 at Tewkesbury, while visiting his brother-in-law Joseph Shapland (c.1774–1837).[29] Stock was a support of the Baptist mission, and according to Thomas Chalmers (1780–1847), was "the pleasantest and most interesting man I know."[30]

Text[31]

My dear Bro^r.

I kn[ow] not what to do. I have two copies only of this Memoir.[32] On[e] [I] must necessarily keep for myself. If I send this und^r cover to the Earl [illegible] [Dr] Stuart will keep it; and I can not send you another.[33] If I s[illegible] it will cost considerable, but you must set it down to [illegible] . Bro^r Hinton I believe or Dyer has sent one to Glasgo[w] [illegible] Edinb. ought to be equally well served; you must let Dr. St[uart] and Mr Innes see it.[34] I am so busy with No xxx of which

---

29 "A layman," *Unitarianism Tried by Scripture and Experience: A Compilation of Treatises and Testimonies in Support of Trinitarian Doctrine and Evangelical Principles. With a General Introduction* (London: Hamilton, Adams, & Co., 1840), 113.

30 William Hanna, *Memoirs of Thomas Chalmers, D.D. LL.D.* (Edinburgh: Edmonston and Douglas, 1867), 1:611.

31 "John Ryland junior Letter," D/RYS (November 29, 1816 [postmark]), Angus Library and Archive, Regent's Park College, Oxford. Permanently loaned by Baiyu Andrew Song.

32 It is almost certain that this memoir refers to John Ryland's *The Work of Faith, the Labour of Love, and the Patience of Hope Illustrated; in the Life and Death of the Reverence Andrew Fuller, Late Pastor of the Baptist Church at Kettering, and Secretary to the Baptist Missionary Society, from It's Commencement, in 1792* (London: Button & Son, 1816). On the text, see Griffith, ed., *Life of Andrew Fuller*, 79–429.

33 Charles Stuart (1746–1826) was the son of James Stuart of Binend (1716–1777), who later twice served as Lord Provost of Edinburgh. Charles was born at Dunearn House near Burntisland in Fife. After ministerial training, Stuart was licensed by the Church of Scotland in London in 1772 and ordained in Cramond Kirk on September 30, 1773. Three years later, due to the influence of Archibald McLean (1733–1812), Stuart embraced credobaptism and resigned his post in May 1776. After briefly organising a Baptist congregation in Edinburgh, Stuart studied medicine at the University of Edinburgh and received his MD degree in 1781. He then practised as a physician in Edinburgh's South Side. Later, Stuart became one of the co-founders of the Royal Society of Edinburgh. He was elected as the President of the Royal College of Physicians of Edinburgh in 1806. He also edited the Edinburgh Quarterly Review from 1798 to 1800. Stuart married Mary Erskine (d. 1817), daughter of John Erskine (1721–1803), in 1773 and had at least eight children, among whom was James Stuart (1775–1849), who was a keen Whig politician (see C.D. Waterston and A. Macmillan Shearer, *Biographical Index of Former Fellows of the Royal Society of Edinburgh 1783–2002. Part II* [Edinburgh: Royal Society of Edinburgh, 2006], 901; Hew Scott, *Fasti Ecclesiæ Scoticanæ: The Succession of Ministers in the Parish Churches of Scotland, from the Reformation, A.D. 1560, to the Present Time. Part I. Synod of Lothian and Tweedale* [Edinburgh: William Paterson; London: John Russell Smith, 1866], 134–135). A copy of Stuart's letter of demission was reprinted as "The Rev. Charles Stuart's Letter of Demission," *Scottish Congregational Magazine* 24 (June 1874): 176–178. Around 1799 Charles Stuart and Andrew Fuller became close friends, and the former became a supporter of the Baptist mission (see Michael D. McMullen and Timothy D. Whelan, eds., *The Diary of Andrew Fuller, 1780–1801*, The Complete Works of Andrew Fuller, vol. 1 [Berlin: de Gruyter, 2016], 196–197, 201–211).

34 James Hinton, minister of New Road Baptist Chapel, Oxford, since 1788, and a supporter of the Baptist mission. From 1815 to 1817, Hinton was the co-secretary with Ryland of the BMS. On Hinton, see John Howard Hinton, *A Biographical Portraiture of the late Rev. James Hinton, M.A.* (Oxford: Bartlett and Hinton; London: B. J. Holdsworth, 1824); Philip Hayden, "The Baptists in Oxford 1656–1819," *Baptist Quarterly* 29.3 (1981): 130–132; Raymond Brown, "'Fear God and honour the King': James Hinton and the Tatham Pamphlet Controversy," in *A Protestant Catholic Church of Christ: Essays on the History and Life of New Road Baptist Church, Oxford*, ed. Rosie Chadwick (Oxford: New Road Baptist Church,

I have written 104 pp. that I have hardly had time to examine it care-fully.[35] I am a little in doubt whether it ought to have been circulated so soon. Our Committee are so disposed to gratify the voracious desire of News, that I think the P. A. will be almost entirely anticipated.[36] Now John Fuller is come to B¹. we shall be able to

2003), 107–135; Tim Grass, "'Walking together in unity and peace and the fear of God': the Challenge of Maintaining Ecumenical Ideals, 1780–1860," in *Protestant Catholic Church*, 148–154; Michael A.G. Haykin, "James Hinton (1761–1823)," in *The British Particular Baptists Volume V More Biographical Essays of Notable British Particular Baptists*, ed. Michael A.G. Haykin and Terry Wolever (Springfield, MO: Particular Baptist Press, 2019), 375–400.

John Dyer (1783–1841) was born on January 3, 1784, at Devizes, Wiltshire, to James Dyer (1743–1797) and Sarah Barton (1746–1833). His father came from Chipping Norton, Oxfordshire, and was an excise officer till 1770. James Dyer experienced conversion under Charles Cole (1733–1813) of Whitchurch, Hampshire. Before his pastoral call, James Dyer was a shopkeeper at Whitchurch until 1782, when he was called to Devizes. After his father's death, John Dyer moved to Broughton, Wiltshire, with an aunt. He then moved with William Steadman (1764–1837) to Plymouth, where the latter first served as a co-pastor with Isaiah Birt (1758–1837), then the sole pastor of the newly-formed Baptist congregation at Liberty Fields (now Pembroke Street) at Plymouth Dock (Devonport). John Dyer was baptised by Steadman in 1800 and joined this new congregation. Dyer was called to minister the Baptist congregation at Howe Street, Plymouth, in 1810, where he served till 1814, when he was called to the Hosier's Lane congregation in Reading. As an advocate for the Baptist mission, Dyer accompanied Andrew Fuller to Scotland. He was chosen as the assistant secretary in 1817 when James Hinton resigned his co-secretaryship. A year later, Dyer was chosen as the first full-time secretary of the BMS, and he moved to Sydenham, London, and remained as a member of Edward Steane's (1792–1882) congregation in Camberwell. Suffering from depression, Dyer was found dead "in a small cistern beneath an archway at the lower part of" his home. With investigation, "a verdict of 'temporary insanity' was returned" ("Memoir of the Rev. John Dyer," *Baptist Magazine* 4 [September 1841]: 437). Also see Ernest A. Payne, *The First Generation: Early Leaders of the Baptist Missionary Society in England and India* (London: Carey, 1936), 120–126; Richard Aldrich, *School and Society in Victorian Britain: Joseph Payne and the New World of Education* (New York: Garland, 1995). On the Baptist congregations at Plymouth, see Baiyu Andrew Song, "Isaiah Birt (1758–1837) and the Baptismal Controversies in Devonshire," *John Bunyan Studies: A Journal of Reformation and Nonconformist Culture* (2024).

William Innes (1770–1855), son of James Innes of Yester (1733–1821) and Maria Hogg. His father ministered at the Yester parish in Gifford for sixty-one years. William Innes was licensed to preach in 1792 and appointed minister of the second charge at Stirling a year later. He was also appointed as the castle chaplain in the same year. Innes married Jane Innes, daughter of the Rev. Dr. Robert Innes of Giffordvale (b. 1730). While in Stirling, Innes became acquainted with Robert Haldane (1764–1842), a landowner in Airthrey. With Haldane's influence, Innes adopted Congregationalist convictions and was deposed from his charge on October 8, 1799. Innes then ministered at the Tabernacle in Dundee in 1800, but due to controversies over credobaptism, he moved to Edinburgh and helped to found the Baptist congregation in Elder Street, Edinburgh, where he laboured for 45 years. While at Edinburgh, Innes sold books. In 1848, Washington College, Pennsylvania, granted Innes an honorary Doctor of Divinity degree. Innes was a supporter for oversea missions. In 1794, after William Wilberforce (1759–1833) advocated for the freedom of missionary enterprises in East India Company controlled area, Robert Haldane, William Innes, Greville Ewing (1767–1841), and David Bogue (1750–1825) proposed a new mission in Benares (see Penny Carson, "The British Raj and the Awakening of the Evangelical Conscience: The Ambiguities of Religious Establishment and Toleration, 1698–1833," in *Christian Missions and the Enlightenment*, ed. Brian Stanley [Grand Rapids, MI: Eerdmans, 2001], 61). Innes also became a supporter of the BMS and friend of Fuller and Ryland (see McMullen and Whelan, eds., *Diary of Andrew Fuller*, 198–200). On Innes' life, see Jonathan Watson, *The Death of his saints precious in the sight of the Lord. A Discourse delivered in Elder Street Chapel on occasion of the death of the Rev. William Innes, D.D., on Sabbath, the 11th of March, 1855. With a Sketch of his Character* (Edinburgh: Innes, 1855); Alfred C. Thomas, *Dr. Innes and his Times. A discourse delivered on occasion of the death of the rev. William Innes, D.D., in Charlotte Chapel, Edinburgh, on Sabbath Evening, March 11, 1855. With a Brief Sketch of his Life* (Edinburgh: William Innes, 1855). Also see William Innes, *Reasons for Separating from the Church of Scotland, in a Series of Letters* (Dundee, 1804).

35 *Periodical Accounts Relative to the Baptist Missionary Society* 6.30 (1816): 1–30. The issue was printed by J.G. Fuller in Bristol and sold by William Button in London. The issue covered the period of January to June 1815, and was published in December 1816. Updates were provided about the Baptist missions in various parts of today's India, Mauritius, Myanmar, Indonesia (Java, Jakarta, and Ambon Island), and Jamaica. There were also updates from the general committee.

36 At the committee meeting on October 15–17, 1816, it was resolved that "no xxx of the P.A. be published as early

bring them out faster a good deal.³⁷ But I almost wish every Convert c^d. go thro a long quarantine before we tell of him. I have some ground of anxiety respecting Kiaba, whose story is so pleasing.

Dr. Stock an eminent Physician, is just converted [from] Socinian^m. and has left Lewin's mead.³⁸ A MS^t Serm. of Dr. Chalmers, lent by my son, thro Rhodes, was of more use than any thing to him.³⁹ The carnal mind is Enmity ag^t. God.⁴⁰ I wish Dr. Ch. w^d. print it.⁴¹ Respects to Mrs. A. and all friends.⁴² I am

---

as possible" ("An Account of the Proceedings of the Baptist Missionary Society," 21). The committee members included: William Burls (chairman, 1763–1837), Isaiah Birt, John Birt (1787–1862), Thomas Blundell, Jr. (1786–1861), Thomas Coles (1779–1840) of Burton-on-the-Water, John Dyer, Robert Hall, Jr., John Keen Hall (d. 1829), Joseph Hall (d. 1822) of Northampton, James Hinton, Thomas Edmonds (1784–1860), Joseph Hughes (1769–1833), Joseph Ivimey (1773–1834), John Jarman (1774–1830), Thomas King (1755–1831), Joseph Kinghorn, James Lomax (1762–1850), Thomas Morgan (1776–1857), William Nicholls (or Nichols, 1762–1835), John Palmer (1768–1823), Thomas Potts (d. 1831) of Birmingham, John Ryland, William Steadman, Saffery, John Yates (1758–1829) of Leicester, and William Winterbother (1763–1829).

37 John Gardiner Fuller, who moved his printing business to Bristol in 1816. He was admitted as a member at Broadmead Baptist chapel on October 19, 1819, and his wife Mary became a member on November 2, 1819. Besides his printing business, Fuller also led the Sunday school, where his apprentice William Knibb (1803–1845) experienced conversion. Notice that Catherine Hall has wrongfully attributed J.G. Fuller as Andrew Fuller's brother, John Fuller, who was the father of Joseph Fuller (Catherine Hall, "William Knibb and the Constitution of the New Black Subject," in *Empire and Others: British Encounters with Indigenous Peoples, 1600–1850*, ed. Martin Daunton and Rick Halpern [Philadelphia: University of Pennsylvania Press, 1999], 308). This mistake was repeated by Hall, in her *Civilising Subjects: Colony and Metropile in the English Imagination, 1830–1867* (Chicago: University of Chicago Press, 2002), 56, and *idem*, "With and Against the Grain," in *How Empire Shaped Us*, ed. Antoinette Burton and Dane Kennedy (London; New York: Bloomsbury, 2016), 72. In Bristol, J.G. Fuller set up his printing shop at St. Augustine's Place.

38 John Edmonds Stock (1774–1835), medical doctor. Lewin's Mead Chapel on Tucker Street was founded as a Presbyterian congregation and later drifted into Unitarianism, which did not prevent its growth. In 1788–1790, the congregation built a new chapel to facilitate increasing attendance. On the chapel, see O.M. Griffiths, "Side Lights on the History of Presbyterian-Unitarianism from the Records of Lewin's Mead Chapel, Bristol," *Transactions of the Unitarian Historical Society* 6 (1935): 116–129.

39 William Rhodes (1792–1856), a graduate of Bristol. See Charles Stanford, *Power in Weakness. Memorials of the Rev. William Rhodes, of Damerham* (London: Jackson and Walford, 1858). Jonathan Edwards Ryland (1798–1866), Ryland's only son. See James Culross, *The Three Rylands: A Hundred Years of Various Christian Service* (London: Elliot Stock, 1897), 95–103. Thomas Chalmers (1780–1847) was a Scottish minister, who was licensed to preach in 1799. After his illness in 1811, Chalmers experienced evangelical conversion and became an advocate for overseas mission. During Fuller's visit in 1813, Chalmers felt "greatly honoured by harbouring" Fuller. Fuller, on the other hand, expressed that "I saw in my dear friend Chalmers a mind susceptible of strong impressions, a capacity of communicating them to others, a thirst for knowledge, and openness to conviction, and a zeal for the promotion of the kingdom of Christ" (Hanna, *Memoirs*, 1:336–337). Chalmers became the minister of the Tron Church, Glasgow, in 1815, and regularly corresponded with John Ryland and Jonathan Edwards Ryland. In 1822, Chalmers visited Ryland in Bristol (see Hanna, *Memoirs*, 1:610–621).

40 Romans 8:7.

41 See Chalmers' sermon, "The Natural Enmity of the Mind Against God," which was published as the 13th sermon in Thomas Chalmers, *Sermons, Preached in the Tron Church, Glasgow* (Glasgow, 1819), 313–333.

42 Christopher Anderson married Esther Athill, "eldest daughter of the Honourable James Athill [1759–1822], Chief Justice of the Island of Antigua" (Anderson, *Life and Letters of Christopher Anderson*, 164). According to Ian Balfour's investigation, though Athill never married, he had at four daughters and six sons by at least four partners. Despite being illegitimate, Athill acknowledged his children and had left legacy in his will. For Esther and Christopher, Athill left £800, in addition to the amount of £1,200 he gave the couple as a wedding gift. Esther (or Hesther) (1784–1824) was the oldest child, and she was born to James Athill and Dorinda, a free Black woman. Dorinda also gave birth to Mary (1785–1824), who

                                                                                              Yours affectly
                                                                                              John Ryland

---

was born on August 14, 1785, baptised on March 24, 1793, and later married Lewis Evans. Esther Athill was born on April 5, 1784, and baptised on March 24, 1793. It is unknown about how Christopher and Esther were met, and when did, if so, Esther received credobaptism. They were married on July 2, 1816, at Paisley, by Robert Burns (1789–1869). Esther gave birth to five children: Esther Eliza, Jane Moubray, Mary Athill, Christopher, and William Ward. However, Esther and all children died with tuberculosis in 1823-4. While mourning for his wife, Anderson wrote *The Genius and Design of the Domestic Constitution, with Its Untransferrable Obligation and Peculiar Advantages* (Edinburgh: Oliver and Boyd, 1826). See Ian Balfour, "Christopher Anderson's Wife and Children," Additional Information, http://ianbalfour.co.uk/wp-content/Additional%20information,%20a%20to%20z/c%20-%20charlie/CHRISTOPHER%20ANDERSON'S%20WIFE%20AND%20CHILDREN.doc (accessed January 9, 2024).

Book Reviews

Andrew Wilson, *Remaking the World: How 1776 Created the Post-Christian West* (Wheaton, IL: Crossway, 2023), 479 pages.

In his recent publication *Remaking the World: How 1776 Created the Post-Christian West*, pastor-theologian Andrew Wilson posits that the eighteenth century, and specifically the year 1776, was the landmark moment for the intellectual changes that became the world we know today. Wilson currently serves as the teaching pastor at King's Church, London, and is also a columnist for *Christianity Today* and a regular online contributor for *The Gospel Coalition*. He is trained in history and theology, holding degrees from Cambridge and King's College, London, but most of his published works have focused on various areas of theology and Christian living. *Remaking the World* is unique among Wilson's books, as it is primarily a work of historical analysis in which he articulates the titular year to be a turning point for some of the most fundamental questions as to the nature of the world and its origins—and by extension how the Christian can now be a faithful witness in light of this worldview shift. Wilson encourages his readers to look to the eighteenth-century church for examples (albeit imperfect ones) of how to thrive in a world that is post-Christian. To this end, he offers his readers a model of how to carefully analyze the past and evaluate its implications for the present from a Christian perspective.

As previously stated, Wilson argues that the year 1776 witnessed several cultural and intellectual transformations (seven to be exact), that completely altered the trajectory of the Western World. In other words, 1776 was the year that made us who we are (7). He uses the acronym WEIRDER to describe the result of these transformations. Compared to the pre-1776 world, our world is now more Western, Educated, Industrialized, Rich, Democratic, Ex-Christian, and Romantic. In the first two chapters of the book, Wilson seeks to demonstrate just how WEIRDER our world is, by focusing on modern developments in psychology, art, and culture that were foreign to the pre-1776 world. The bulk of the book (chapters 3–9) analyzes each of the respective transformations that the year 1776 witnessed: rapid globalization (chapter 3), the American Revolution (chapter 4), the rise of Enlightenment philosophy (chapter 5), religious skepticism (chapter 6), the Industrial Revolution (chapter 7), the rise of Romanticism (chapter 8), and the Great Enrichment (chapter 9). In the last two chapters of the book, Wilson seeks to bridge the gap between history and the cotemporary church. First, in chapter 10 he probes the question of how eighteenth-century believers responded to their rapidly changing world, and he argues that the celebration of grace, the pursuit of freedom, and an articulation of Christian truth gave the church its direction towards a post-secular future (264). Then, in chapter 11, he argues that those same three commitments, though not a foolproof strategy for success, will help to strengthen the contemporary church as it seeks to be a faithful witness to the WEIRDER world it finds itself in.

In his analysis of the eighteenth-century world, with all its changes and complexities, Wilson demonstrates an impressive breadth and depth of knowledge. He clearly has read widely in this subject area, and he has drawn attention to historical factors, such as developments in art and economics, that could easily be overlooked by historians seeking to understand this period. Wilson is to be commended for his research into these areas. He is also to be commended for his careful handling of the intricacies of historical dynamics. For example, he recognizes the paradoxical reality that the church has often been indirectly responsible for in the social, intellectual, and economic developments that have unwittingly given herself cause for concern (245). Furthermore, he recognizes that the challenges faced by the contemporary church are quite different from those faced by the eighteenth-century church. This recognition leads him to conclude that "there is no strategy identified in the late eighteenth century that would transform the fortunes of the church today, if only we had the courage to implement it" (276). Nevertheless, he does not shy away from encouraging his readers to follow the example of the eighteenth-century church in each of the three commitments outlined above. In all this, Wilson demonstrates how Christians should think about the past and draw implications from it while remaining mindful of its many complexities.

Perhaps the biggest weakness of the book lies with the thesis itself, potentially overreaching in its stated claim. It is one thing to say that the late eighteenth century was incredibly significant in the course of Western history. Many scholars of the period would likely agree with that assessment. However, it is another thing to say that the year 1776, "more than any other year in the last millennium" made the world what it is today (7). There are times when Wilson's argument makes this contention seem entirely plausible, but at other points it falls short. For example, in his chapter on the Enlightenment, Wilson notes that Immanuel Kant (1724–1804) produced a preliminary outline in 1776 that would evolve into *The Critique of Pure Reason* (1781), a work "that would turn philosophy on its head" (123). The importance of this publication in the course of Western intellectual history is indisputable, but as to the extent that the drafting of a mere preliminary outline constitutes a "major intellectual development" is debatable. Thus, this narrow scope of Wilson's thesis leaves the reader with the need to discern the strength of evidence. Nevertheless, Wilson has made a compelling argument that will certainly generate fruitful scholarly discourse.

Those seeking to answer the critical questions outlined at the beginning of this review would be wise to read *Remaking the World*. This book is undoubtedly valuable as a work of historical scholarship, but its real value lies in its attempt draw together the past and the present in a responsible way. Wilson not only helps his readers understand how the modern world has come to be, but he also provides them with a vision for Christian faithfulness in the face of that world and its many challenges.

Zachary Williams
The Southern Baptist Theological Seminary
Louisville, Kentucky

Valerie Smith, *Rational Dissenters in Late Eighteenth-Century England: "An Ardent Desire of Truth"* (Rochester, NY: Boydell, 2021), 219 pages.

Rational Dissenters is a posthumous work by the late Valerie Smith who passed away in 2019 with this work nearly complete, having spent much of her life teaching history and engaged in archival research. In this publication, she provides a fascinating study of how this unorthodox minority emerged and distinguished itself toward the end of the Long Eighteenth Century—arguing that the theological beliefs of these more peculiar Dissenters became the impetus for their political engagement. Stressing a gap in research previously identified through the works of John Seed and Patrick Collinson, she demonstrates that scholarship has barely scratched the surface concerning the theological underpinnings of the Rationalists (9–10). She states, "No study to date has focused exclusively and in depth on the complexities of identity among Rational Dissenters, nor on the identities ascribed to them by others of different religious sympathies in the late eighteenth century" (16). By engaging with the theological beliefs of these Dissenters the complex political theology that they held may be better understood.

Smith asserts three main doctrines which give cohesion and distinction to the Rational Dissenters: the absence of original sin, denial of the atonement, and a rejection of predestination (63). She further describes how the Rational Dissenters cultivated this sense of identity by negation through having a "keen awareness of what they were not" (103). Thus, while these misfits are often neatly sheltered under the designations of Socinianism and Arianism, Smith articulates that this unorthodox system functioned as the means for developing a political ideology, as they had formalized such an ideology upon the pretense of anti-trinitarianism. Flowing out of this, the Rationalists could compromise on matters such as abolition, morality, Scriptural authority and reliability, mode and purpose of baptism, regulative types of prayer, and the perception of Christ's humanity (41, 79, 87, 89). Here Smith pulls on the common thread of a type of humanism, noting "the rejection of original sin led to optimism about humanity's capacity for improvement," which shaped a high moral ethic for which they revered "Christ's teaching rather than his crucifixion" or atonement (50, 56). The concern of the church, and its fight before the public conscience, was for the "the moral reformation of the individual" (86). The ability of humans to articulate and reach a supreme moral code in this life led the Rational Dissenters to uniformly view "Public worship as a means of intellectual improvement" wherein the theological views would be a means to "buttress a tenacious work of progressivism" (65, 99).

What Smith makes particularly clear through her analysis is the evolution of these Rationalist minorities into what was essentially an amalgamated denomination. She shines much needed light on how these divergent perspectives reluctantly sheltered themselves under the Unitarian label, "unhelped by other nonconformists" (187, 201). Lacking viability on their own and crippled by what may be considered an ostentatious intellectualization, Smith notes their ineffectiveness for building a base (189). Without the evangelistic weight concerning depravity and atonement, the Rational mission was merely moral education. However, Smith shows that their target audience was not the poor or uneducated (193). With only two poorly publicized societies that modelled themselves after the Particular Baptists for propagation, their evangelism boiled down to returning Christians to the "purity of primitive Christianity uncorrupted by post-apostolic additions" and to affirming a universalism based on the negation of atonement (145, 200, 217). The legacy of the movement embodied the proverb: the enemy of my enemy is my friend. Those groups divergent from the Orthodox Dissenters shaped themselves around the idea of toleration—and as the major common ideals developed those subsidizing the movement organized around them. Thus, the name eventually took on a non-dogmatic label of Unitarianism (181, 197), which emphasized an inalienable right to conscience would necessitate a freedom of religion (131).

One area of value to readers of *JAFS* is Smith's engagement—limited though it may be—with Baptists, such as Daniel Turner (1710–1798), John Macgowan (1726–1780), Abraham Booth (1734–1806), Caleb Evans (1737–1791), Joseph Jenkins (1743–1819), John Ryland (1753–1825), and Andrew Fuller (1754–1815). Smith points out that the theological articulation of Rational Dissenters gave Particular Baptists a means for utilizing such "precise details" as a formula for orthodox defensives (33, 38–39). Among the Particular Baptists, their counterarguments were capable of building evangelistic conclusions for their own cause. The intellectual tête-à-tête came through a multitude of letters and pamphlets as Rational Dissenters made their positions clearer. Ryland accused the Socinians of being "irrational Christians," playing on the label of their movement, while Fuller and Macgowan were compelled to reveal the Rational Dissenter's lacklustre view of Scripture (78–79). Fuller's remarkable ability to combat the highbrow assertions of the Socinians meant repeated and highly structured engagement (35). Following the riots attributed to Joseph Priestly (1733–1804), Daniel Turner called for orthodox Dissenters (specifically the Baptists) to affirm their loyalty to the government, as Smith notes, to further distinguish themselves theologically as well as politically from these Rational Dissenters (147).

Weaknesses in the book are more for lack of space than for advancement of her argument. Smith gives minimal substantiation to her claim regarding a failed evangelistic methodology on behalf of the Rational Dissenters. She likewise examines little as to why their educational endeavors were insufficient. While Smith argues for what motivated the political actions of the Rational Dissenters, she does not actually address their successes or failures. Even so, Smith provides an incredible bibliographical register of Rational Dissenting subscribers as well as authors through her appendices. Likewise, the mapping of locations and concentrations of the movement help identify its physicality and influence as the Rational Dissenters merge into the Unitarian denomination. The landscape of Dissent in England's long Eighteenth Century is made all the more navigable thanks to Valerie Smith's contribution.

Christopher Österbrock
FBC Wellsboro
Wellsboro, PA

Ruth Gouldbourne and Anthony Cross, *The Story of Bristol Baptist College: Three Hundred Years of Ministerial Formation* (Eugene, OR: Pickwick Publications, 2022), 215 pages.

Anthony Cross departed this life to be with the Lord in July 2021. He was an important Baptist leader and historian, directing the Centre for the Baptist History and Heritage at Regent's Park College, Oxford, and serving as a professor at the University of Oxford. He published dozens of books and essays on issues ranging from Baptist sacramentalism, to ecumenism, to education. Cross passed away before he was able to complete his history of Bristol Baptist College, therefore Professor Gouldbourne has admirably collected and presented three volumes of Cross's "raw material" of research in this compact book. She notes that, had Cross been able to complete his work, the book would be much improved, but calls it a book written "for the family," that is, for the Bristol Baptist College community who will directly benefit from reading this history (xi).

The book proceeds in chronological order from the school's founding and then at intervals of the subsequent three centuries of the college's life. The narrative surveys the major leaders and students, taking note of key developments in British Baptist life and educational practices. A key theme that drives the book is the continuity of school characteristics and culture from 1720 to the present day. This book is distinguished in the warmth of its tone, as it is clearly written by one who loves and believes in "the Bristol Tradition." Anyone looking to understand Baptist educational practices and ministerial training across the centuries will find much to glean in this volume.

A potential weakness of the book is its agenda to find a certain ecumenism and inclusivism from the college's earliest days (14–15, 28–29). Such a theme is not objectionable in itself, but such statements lack evidence. In reading primary source materials, especially from the long Eighteenth Century, one may find a willingness to cooperate with non-Calvinists and non-Baptists in limited spheres (such as in abolishing the slave trade). However, this book frequently minimizes the doctrinal and denominational particularity of the early work of the college.

Along with some historical inaccuracies and infelicitous typographical mistakes, one regrettable error in the book is its confusion of John Collett Ryland (1723–1792), with his son, John Ryland, Jr. (1753–1825). It was Ryland, Jr. who succeeded Caleb Evans as principal of the college, yet the book conflates the biographical information of the father and son (20–21). For example, the book notes that Ryland Jr. studied under Bernard Foskett, who died in 1758, while Ryland, Jr. was only five years old. The authors should not be severely faulted, since confusing the Rylands has not been infrequent through the years of Baptist scholarship.

While there are several wrinkles that could have been ironed out, the book is a delight to read, it tells important story about the Bristol tradition, and it rightly honors the final scholarly work out of the late Anthony Cross. At Cross's request, the book has no footnotes, endnotes, or bibliography, in the hope that someone else might take up the task of researching and writing a complete and critical history of the college. Given the circumstances, Professor Goulbourne is to be heartily commended for seeing this project to publication.

Garrett M. Walden
Grace Heritage Church
Auburn, AL

Michael A.G. Haykin and Jerry Slate, *Loving God and Neighbor with Samuel Pearce* (Bellingham, WA: Lexham Press, 2019), 166 pages.

This instalment in *The Lived Theology* series by Lexham Press provides an overview of the life and impact of Samuel Pearce (1766–1799) among the Particular Baptists toward the latter part of the eighteenth century. As one of the twelve men who signed the agreement at Kettering in 1792 to form the Baptist Missionary Society, a contemporary study on Pearce is apropos for the readers of *JAFS*—whose influence is especially apparent on the namesake of this journal, having produced himself a memoir in his honor after his passing. This is notable as Samuel Pearce lived a relatively short life, yet (as the authors mention in the opening words of the introduction) he "packed decades of spiritual maturity into a few short years of life" (1).

The two authors weave together their contributions into this composition by first highlighting the trajectory of Pearce's life into the pastorate (chapters 1–4), and then detail some of the major contours of his ministry and spirituality (chapters 5–11). The opening chapters trace Samuel Pearce's journey from understanding his own spiritual state apart from Christ, the challenges of being a new convert, to his maturation and instruction at Bristol Baptist Academy. Michael Haykin recounts that it was not merely the intellectual instruction that shaped Pearce during his time at the institution, but also the cultivating environment for a love of Christ by Caleb Evans (1737–1791) and the friendships with fellow student Josiah Evans (1760–1792) and William Steadman (1964–1837) (20, 22).

The fifth chapter transitions to the woman who would become his closest friend, his wife Sarah Hopkins (1771–1804). Sarah herself had been part of the Bristol Academy sphere through her alumnus father and close friend of the aforementioned Caleb Evans. This theme of friendship that marked the life of Pearce (and indicated in the title of this work) is increasingly brought to the fore by the authors as they survey the various aspects of Pearce's life. In some chapters this theme is readily apparent, such as the role of pastor and need to love the souls to whom they preach (70), his understanding that "while truth must be unapologetically preached and taught it must be done so in love" (98), and the humility in trusting his friends' decision not to send him to India as a missionary despite his own desires (112).

In another chapter, however, the theme of geniality is not as readily apparent but is still discernible is an overview of his political persuasions. Pearce lived in an "age of profound religious persecution" (50) and the tumult felt by the revolutions in America and France (the latter of which initially had the sympathy of Dissenters [54]) had incentivized the government to establish restrictive policies concerning religious affairs for the sake of civil stability. This had obvious ramifications and conflicts with the missionary efforts. Yet Pearce alongside his colleagues sought to thread opposition against civil governments that hindered such efforts while also disciplining missionaries who supported "incendiary politics that spawned and fuelled revolution" (61) He was not a political activist at heart and warning against an overinvestment in political controversies (a sentiment shared by Andrew Fuller in his work "Backslider" in which he attributed spiritual malformation to such obsession), but Pearce's love for humanity allowed for some political appeal.

This work is wonderful additional to the library of those looking for an additional

Baptist resources and primers, especially on lesser-known figures. The book could be read in a single sitting—the chapters themselves are easily consumable in small portions both in length and topical nature. It fits well into the series nomenclature, entering into the life of the reader as it encourages and challenges personal growth.

Caleb Anthony Neel
The Southern Baptist Theological Seminary
Louisville, KY

www.ingramcontent.com/pod-product-compliance
Lightning Source LLC
Chambersburg PA
CBHW030557080526
44585CB00012B/412